GW01003604

35p

$17\frac{2}{6}$p

IN TOUCH

IN TOUCH

John Steinbeck IV

ANDRE DEUTSCH

FIRST PUBLISHED 1969 BY
ANDRE DEUTSCH LIMITED
105 GREAT RUSSELL STREET
LONDON WC1
COPYRIGHT © 1968, 1969 BY JOHN STEINBECK IV

ALL RIGHTS RESERVED

PRINTED IN GREAT BRITAIN BY
LOWE AND BRYDONE (PRINTERS) LTD., LONDON

233 96137 2

"The Importance of Being Stoned in Vietnam" by John Steinbeck IV and "Who Me? I'm a Sociologist" by Tom Kelly (Copyright © 1968 by Washington Magazine Inc.) first appeared in the *Washingtonian* magazine.

The quotation from the *Tao Te Ching: The Way of Life* by Lao Tzu is taken from Raymond B. Blakney's translation, published by permission of the New American Library, Inc.

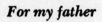
For my father

Contents

INTRODUCTION

I want to explain how I came to write this book. It might well be subtitled *A Year in the Life of One Young American*. Certainly each part of this past year or so has been inexorably linked with the preceding part. But, insofar as the "writing" part is concerned, it was triggered by the fact that my first published effort was a magazine article about marijuana in Vietnam. The subject might well have been some other, but an editor happened to hear me talking about this and asked for the article. From then on, because of a series of events (including my being arrested and charged with possession of the drug), I became closely involved with marijuana as a topic and a liability.

When it was first suggested that I develop the article into a book, which would be all about marijuana, I refused. Public opinion, the news media, and extensive research and medical commentary have made it difficult, if not impossible, to write about marijuana without falling into the usual overstated posture either for or against the use of it. However, for any open-minded young person marijuana is an easy subject on which to be outspoken, since it involves so many contradictions readily apparent in our overmedicated American society. The image arises of a mother getting so excited while warning her son against the evils of marijuana—the oldest of relaxants—that she has to take a tranquilizer to calm down. In many ways marijuana is almost the perfect subject for any eager, socially aware youth to get involved with in his search for a way to wash the universe free of its moral contradictions and hypocrisies. Traditionally, and I suppose forever, it seems to be the fate and sometimes the stimulating function of youth to spot the cracks in the smooth vinyl reality which older generations insist is the master design on which all their realistic thinking is based.

Part of this tradition also permits the youth to go on spotting these flaws in the accepted order without ever having to see the cracks in the new order he is presenting. Still, this bit of social foolery has enough charm to keep things going forward, and once in a while something like child labor is abolished. Perhaps, in another few years, with youth becoming increasingly sophisticated, the children will turn full swing and riot in the streets protesting their lack of employment. This is only to say that I don't present myself here as the changeless voice of social truth, since my age alone is evidence enough for me to be absolutely sure my thoughts are no more timeless than the ones I would take issue with. And I am sensitive to what Hoffer calls the "juvenilization on an almost global scale" which is evident around the world today. I do not want to offer juvenile, simplistic answers to complex problems.

Another problem in writing about marijuana was that I had already talked about it enough to bore myself to death. As a result of my name and arrest I found myself talking about marijuana all day every day. This is pretty deadly for someone who just wants to smoke it from time to time. I found myself endlessly going through my well-used list of justifications and anecdotes illustrating my particular feelings about marijuana. Each phrase would lead to the next one, like an over-rehearsed medley which at least to me was obviously too well remembered by the performer. From Georgetown cocktail parties to Senate testimony the word "marijuana" had developed an annoying ring to it. Those who use it, of course, rarely call it by that name. Endless euphemisms—grass, pot, weed, dope—serve the purpose, just as tobacco or alcohol users have a variety of terms for common usage. Even the most critical person should be able to understand that marijuana (again, like tobacco or alcohol) is an extremely boring topic of discussion to the people who use the stuff. It is excessively talked about by novice users. This turning-off effect comes when the subject of marijuana is the only thing being discussed, illustrating a severe poverty of interest, whether it is talked about by teachers, parents, generals, or doctors. Of course the medical profession (our ultimate protectors, if protection is possible) finds itself in the worst double-bind. The only way teachers and parents and generals know how to stamp out marijuana use is to promote more education on the subject. And yet the highly educated and informed medical profession contains the highest incidence of drug users. This kind of fact can provide some sardonic amusement to marijuana smokers.

However, since I believed marijuana was a perfect subject to use as metaphor and tool in examining much else, I decided I should write about it. I know that any topic, be it marijuana, liquor, sex, war, religion, or politics, is bound to open up serial points of view on other matters. Although my ideas on any subject are necessarily youthful, they do exist, and I know that once embarked upon any kind of communication many of them will out.

In order to make my life and my attitudes more understandable I have described some of what happened to me as a soldier in Vietnam. The last year of my Army hitch was certainly the most differentiated year of my life. Because of this I feel a particular need to explain chronologically how I landed in this pseudo-expert role where I was recounting, not so much what is right or wrong about marijuana, but rather my thoughts on what's with marijuana.

After my arrest concluded in a not-guilty verdict in trial by jury, I had thought I was through spending my mental energy in long bouts of facts and contradictions concerning the use of the plant. However, one day soon after the trial, I received a call from the Senate Subcommittee on Juvenile Delinquency and was asked to clarify questions about marijuana as an expert on the subject. A great weight was taken off my mind when I realized I didn't have to defend my views, as in court, but merely relate them. I had covered the route from accused criminal to respected expert with no stops along the way. I am grateful for this ludicrous metamorphosis, and now I find myself welcoming the opportunity to crystallize all the fragments of this journey from the somewhat sordid to the somewhat sublime as a setting for this book.

Because I am identified always, even in the briefest of captions, as my father's son, I feel a need to explain where I stand in regard to my father. I cannot say that I have grown accustomed to wearing *his* name; it is also my own. He gave it to me; I didn't choose it. Nevertheless I have been aware all my life that it is a name sufficiently unusual that it immediately connects me to him and places me primarily as "the son of the novelist" before anything else may be said about me. Further, since the themes of his novels are so rooted in the American scene, he seems to have become a kind of American-conscience figure. Therefore my youthful opinions on any social subject are invariably compared to what my father might think of that same subject.

Perhaps this will continue all my life; I would hope it does not. But it may, unless I decide to choose some pseudonym. This is a question I have considered at length. Obviously, as other children of famous parents have found out, there are both advantages and disadvantages. But the idea of going anonymous, as it were, seems a fraudulent and futile subterfuge. Since I was seventeen I have been on my own entirely. "Steinbeck" was the name stitched on my Army uniform, and I do not think it helped or hurt my ability to be drafted and sent to Vietnam like any other soldier. As this book will show, I did not deliberately choose to be a "writer" in the sense of selecting my father's vocation.

There is no doubt in my mind that my father is like any father in that he would prefer to have a son who did well in school, who conformed to the routine manners and morals of society, who took no risks—in short, who didn't make waves. I have never been that kind of a son and I know this has caused a great deal of anxiety for my father, mother, and brother, and the rest of my family. However, I am not ashamed of what I do and I don't think my family would want me to be. There is also no doubt I inherited my father's nature; we both like to communicate. It has seemed probable to me for several years that I would end up having a career in some aspect of the communications industry, perhaps in TV, until this series of recent events put me in a position where I found myself specifically *writing,* putting words on paper.

When I was a child, and wrote anything at all, my parents and their friends thought it was cute—"just like his dad." But the difference between writing and saying something may sometimes suddenly push open the door and let in a blast of chilly air. Then one is compelled to have an opinion on whether the kid's writing is still sentimentally endearing, adolescently awkward, or downright unpleasant—even, perhaps, good. Maybe I am not capable of being a writer. But I must admit to being occasionally overcome by the possible delusion that I have something to say, quite apart from being my father's son.

The actual elapsed time of this chronicle, or journal, is clearly recent and brief enough to show I have not been considering writing as a profession for very long. When people talk to me as if I were a Writer—as I think a Writer is— the word itself has an odd sound to my ear. I remember and see my father as a Writer, as a man who works diligently at his skills and his art. I can hardly identify with such devotion. Rather than force myself to conform to a style which in most cases is only born of long experience, with continued exposure to the craft, I have chosen whatever form of expression seemed best to me for the ideas included in any one section. If there is no unified or coherent literary style it is because there is a still-changing mind behind those thoughts and words. Having mainly my own ideas, impressions, anecdotes, and analyses to offer, I will not impose too much on the reader's willingness to read another's words. But where I felt it to be appropriate I have quoted and used whatever documentation seemed in keeping with my sense of the book's continuity.

Jemez Springs, New Mexico   **J.S.**
1968

ONE

AT WAR

I

When I arrived in Saigon in June 1966, the Buddhist revolt
was just subsiding, and control of the Unified Buddhist
Church was going back to the Republic's Army. It wasn't
quite settled, however, when I took my first bus ride from
my office to the Hotel Ky Son, which had been assigned to me
as living quarters. As we drove along I couldn't help being
awed by how much there was to see and stare at. Every inch
of the streets held a sight that would hypnotize me. They
weren't particularly wonderful, or good, or bad, just so new.

The newness of the Asian noises filling the air, and the
smells that mingled shit and ambrosia, marijuana and incense, enlivened my mind. Every minute was filled with what
seemed to me to be more seconds and milliseconds than an
entire day had possessed when I was bored and waiting to
leave the States. Where before things had been usual, and
un-inked by my consciousness because of their normality,
now my mind grabbed and savored everything that was
thrown at it with the avidity of a child unknowingly memo-
rizing all the shiny metal objects worn into the city streets
and asphalt of his neighborhood. They don't exist to the people who move over them a thousand times a day.

The bus ride seemed to take wonderful hours. In front of
us I saw a small fire burning in the middle of the street we
were approaching. The fire was being fueled by lovely bits of
colored paper and decorations. There were children standing

near, ringing bells, and brightly dressed people of all ages milled around. The bus driver, who was Vietnamese and spoke no English, began to look frightened and started to howl quietly to himself. The bus started to roll over the fire, and almost at once people came from nowhere and crowded in like a wall on all sides of us. This was no longer a quaint little celebration, but a Buddhist demonstration. They had put up their altars all over town to force the government to "walk on the church." It was a typical passive-resistance confrontation, at which the Buddhists excel.

As soon as the people had us trapped they started stoking the fire under the bus while they banged and rattled the sides of the General Motors funeral pyre. The tiny driver went immediately into a form of hysterics that was to become more familiar. Despite his show of sincere and deep emotional disturbance, the bus stayed where it was and the flames under it grew higher. I was sitting transfixed in the seat next to the driver. Rocks were hitting the bus, and the driver just got more silently hysterical. Not having the wit to be intimidated, I pushed him aside, put the bus in first gear, and began pushing the celebrants at about half a mile an hour. They kept clinging to the heavy wire fencing that covered the windows, fencing that was specifically built to keep out rocks, grenades, and holiday crowds. We cleared the fire, and no one felt passionate enough that day to fling himself under the wheels of the bus. With curses and bells banging, the trip to my hotel continued. I had been in the Republic of Vietnam about five hours.

I asked for military service in Vietnam because I thought I wanted to know what was going on there, rather than hear the name mentioned a thousand times a day by people who had never breathed Vietnam's air. There were those who protested America's position there without any valid basis with which I could really agree. There were some who supported our position there without reasonable reasons other than those continually spouted dialectics born years ago, the lessons of which had died with the history that gave them birth.

My family heritage had been a rich and wise one. Often I had felt more allied to adults than I did to my own generation. I think back now and smile at what must have seemed to other young people to be my pseudo-sophistication. Whereas their idea of sophistication led them to evade the draft by whatever means, mine led me to accept the draft. I was not quite ready to enlist; that would have seemed unsophisticated to me. But if I were called I knew that I would go. If this was the war for my generation I would accept it, let it happen to me, and also satisfy my curiosity about Vietnam and myself. Perhaps I would find answers there which would seem more than just mouthings.

So I was drafted, put through the usual basic training at Fort Bliss, and emerged ready for action. On leave, after basic, I was aloof and alone when I told my friends that I had volunteered for Vietnam. I got in some furious arguments because I was upset with the large numbers of young people who seemed to refuse to accept the fact that Vietnam even existed, beyond the knowledge that they didn't want to go there. It also seemed to me that in many cases they didn't want to do anything. Too many of them were hiding unhappily in school, spending a lot of time figuring out how to stay in school with the least pain, or even the most joy.

I was fortunate to have been able to travel a great deal in my boyhood and I had grown to appreciate the image of my country even as seen from abroad. I felt self-consciously pleased to be American. A vague but powerful sense of responsibility and an eager curiosity about myself demanded that I get to Vietnam as soon as possible. I received my travel orders in minimum time for Army personnel, and I was on my way with the questions which had stormed my head. I also had some answers well in my head when I arrived in Vietnam, since I had already formed some of the conclusions I would need in order to maintain a purposeful equilibrium as an American soldier there. What I needed was the ammunition of direct experience to give these conclusions weight and supply them with references. Secretly, even to myself, I had no intention of letting the glory of my forefathers sink under the weight of a pacifist's banner.

With my hawk's talons sharpened by Army training, at first I buried much of what fell within the realm of my awareness so that I could support the appropriate beliefs. With a zeal born of wanting my country, and myself, to be doing the right thing, all that I allowed myself to see, hear, and feel in any political sense reinforced my set of opinions.

But the war in Vietnam is such a mixed affair. I didn't land there with any sense of arriving at the front. It was more like what arriving in London during the '40's must have been like. There were many times in Saigon when I felt completely like a tourist and I could respond to the atmosphere with no sense of being a soldier in uniform. I had not expected that to happen, although I had some ideas about what sort of life I would make for myself when I requested duty there. Knowing my own tendencies and appetites, I knew at least what the pace and pulse of living there would mean to me.

When I stepped off the plane at Ton Son Nhut from the cool sterile air of a Pan American 707 into the June steam, I felt that I had come home by going someplace else. What most of the passengers faced with dread seemed to me to be a paradise of potential crystallized experience. It is a fixed law of organic evolution that those primitive animals that put on armor would never again escape that shell. The turtle, armadillo, and all the other mammals, reptiles, and especially insects that mutated to wear a protective coat to shield themselves against other forces in nature would never again be freed by mutation from that dead end. Their state and position in biological time stopped, and they have remained unchanged for millions of years. When the waves of impressions of Southeast Asia hit me on the stairs of the plane, I understood that this biological law was intellectually and emotionally true as well. In searching for examples to back up my newfound dialectic, it seemed to be true that people were frozen as well when they chose to close themselves in from their environment, whether physical or perceived. Growth could only come by exposing all of me to all that came near to touch me. It was soon to become a compulsion to the point where I would throw myself in front of any wave that attracted me. Even if I was attracted by its horror as well as its beauty, I wanted to jump in front of each possible experience and see how far I would be tumbled and changed. More than once it nearly killed me. Knowing the spirit of mutation, though, I know as well that it made my life the way it is now, as it also changed my ability to perceive a change in the first place.

Before I was drafted I was a radio and television announcer in Palm Springs, California. To the Army this meant "broadcast specialist," and I was assigned to the Armed Forces Radio and Television in Vietnam. There were about seventeen men in the unit when I arrived. When I left a year later there were over two hundred men serving the huge network of broadcast entertainment that was designed to let the troops transcend their immediate environment.

For the most part my experiences were filled with the million endearing things of mankind that become so obvious in a war zone. I spent about half my time on duty in Saigon, and the other half I spent moving around various forward positions. It is easy to be caught up in the feeling of brotherhood when, with fellow soldiers, you build a fantastic Christmas tree out of barbed wire and decorate it with grenades and ammunition belts. Living with the Montagnards, playing with their children, brings out the warmest side in any young American. I saw myself and my friends overcompensate with the "better half" of ourselves, as if making sublime concessions to ourselves, filling our eyes with our goodness as if to blot out the sad and absurd concept that we were in a position to be good or bad to begin with. Doubt has the most revealing calling card. It took a while before I realized that within those tokens of virtue was the key to what was most certainly going on in the lives of the so-called "enemy" as well. To avoid analyzing what we Americans were really doing there my mind was easily sidetracked by the colorful and most often inspiring outer shell of the conflict.

Because of the very gradual buildup of American effort in Vietnam, from the American soldier's point of view the war had a very definite evolution from day to day. I remember hearing stories when I first got into the Army from soldiers who had been stationed in Vietnam around 1963. The war was quite different when I arrived in 1966, and it changed dramatically during the year I was there. In the early days, my Vietnamese friends told me, it was like a casual people's war; brothers from the same village, though they were on opposing sides, might meet in a village bar at night to talk over the day's events. They would trade control of a road or supply route with far more diplomacy than we seemed to muster after we turned the war into an American economic morality play. The original military advisory teams, which in the countryside were made up of fifteen to twenty men, had a very small role. But by 1965 the Military Advisory Group (MAG) became the Military Assistance Command—Vietnam (MACV), which had its headquarters in Saigon. This command unit, headed by General Westmoreland, took control of all Allied forces which were to come to Southeast Asia as the buildup continued. When I got my orders for Vietnam, assigning me to the radio-television station in Saigon, I became a member of MACV. Since the chain of command is very important to the freedom a soldier might enjoy, it is necessary to outline briefly how the system works in Vietnam.

These days most Vietnam policy comes directly from Washington, but in the earlier days of the war the MAG group received its directives in more leisurely fashion from its superior commander, who was Admiral U. S. Grant Sharp, United States Commander of all our forces in the Pacific theater of operations. However, Armed Forces Radio and Television was an Information Activity of the Department of Defense, and even in Vietnam its policies always came directly from Washington. Our unit was under the guidance of MACV, but our close association with Washington and the DOD, combined with the fear of a superior authority so pervasive in the military mind, allowed the members of AFRT to ignore the commands of many officers. We even carried passes allowing us to be out after curfew if we were moving from one place to another in the line of duty. This, of course, was never the way the pass was used. Because of the small size of the broadcast operation that I was assigned to, in late 1966 it was still the gentle fate of broadcast specialists to remain stationed in Saigon for the duration of their year in Vietnam. When the buildup became more intense, a few months after I arrived, this easy duty was coming to an end even in our unit. My first weeks in Vietnam provided me with a quickly fleeting view of what life had been like for the Saigon Warrior.

Many of the old days were spent going from the hotel to bars, to the radio-television station, to the old French golf course, to more bars, and then back to the hotel. After being in Vietnam for a while, most soldiers rented an apartment to play house with a domestically minded bar girl. Though the Information Office was naturally just one of thousands of the support assignments making up MACV, this life of vapid luxury became the preoccupation of most of the Allied and American troops in Saigon.

When most people think about a war they no doubt imagine hundreds of thousands of soldiers away from home all with the same goal in mind militarily. Many people realize what a huge amount of paperwork goes on in addition to the combat or mechanized support. But very few have been exposed to that branch of endeavor devoted to molding the participants' thoughts about what they're doing there to begin with. This is the function of the Information Office. When the outside world is brought in, it's called the Public Information Office and its members are designated PIO's. As American involvement escalated, the Information Office in Vietnam expanded logarithmically to fill the void and to supply appropriate answers to the thousands of questions the new troops brought with them. For AFRT this meant primarily more news and entertainment.

For the Information Office as a whole the task included informing the civilian news media as to just what happened and what was now taking place in Vietnam. Every day at five o'clock in Saigon the MACV Information Office gave its daily briefing on all military actions of the preceding twenty-four-hour period of report. This was known generally as "The Five O'Clock Follies." In other wars the military arm of society was largely allowed to perform its aggressive function and to account to no one other than its commanders. Their moves and tactics didn't have to be daily justified and explained. They were soldiers primarily anyway, and no one expected them to do anything but fight. Today the military has become paralyzed in deceit through their Information Offices. The deceit wouldn't have existed if the military had been left to the skills of war. But as America's conscience grew with her might, and the media rose to the task, the self-conscious concept of public relations was futilely applied to a fraternity assembled for violence. I'm sure the military doesn't think this is futile in spite of the fact that the credibility gap widens in direct proportion to the amount of information produced.

The radio and television facilities weren't very large when I first arrived in Saigon. There were some relay stations built upcountry to carry the radio signal farther north than the Saigon transmitter would allow, but even with this assist our AM radio signal only covered about a third of the country, and the FM signal never got out of Saigon. Television programs were broadcast for three hours in the evening from a plane circling over Saigon. Extensive plans were being made to set up mobile TV and radio sites throughout the country in the form of transmitting trailer vans. The vans, eight in all, were to come between the end of 1966 and June 1967, and one by one they were to be installed and maintained by a crew of nine of us broadcast specialists, an officer, and an NCO. It was certain that the soft days were over for AFRT, although the plans would not be ready for a couple of months. My early life in Vietnam was spent making the most of the last days of luxury in the disappearing gentlemen's war of Southeast Asia.

Though I was to be under fire a number of times in Vietnam the story of combat in this war is hardly mine to tell. When I was involved with the infantry it was in the capacity of newsman for AFRT, which is not at all to be confused with the role of the hundreds of thousands of Americans who had combat as their sole jobs. There is little doubt their story will be told in letters, films, books for many years to come. I spent my last week in Vietnam being mortared in our television station in Hué, but most of my memories are from another part of the war, in many ways the strangest part.

Some of the areas that make up the myriad parts of Saigon represent the end result of recent political and material changes in the country. In no way could they be called artificial, though. The Ton Son Nhut air base became a city in itself for the Air Force personnel in Saigon. The very fact that so many troops arrived and departed from this one little plot of earth became a status quo within the fluctuation of the district. As modern machines moved into what used to be rice paddies, the original environment altered, and in turn changed the military as it adapted to what it had created. There were some bizarre manifestations of this process. After the air base had started to build into the huge facility it is, a community of small whorehouses, stores, and laundries sprouted up around the complex. Many of the troops first sent to Vietnam for the original advisory teams were transferred there from other Asian duty. Most came from Okinawa or Korea. With the larger buildup thousands of American troops came from the bases throughout the Orient. With their Pavlovian linguistic thought associations most of these GI's were certain they could get their ideas across with any Asian slang they happened to know—after all, the Vietnamese were Orientals. They assaulted this fringe of Asia with whatever part of the Orient they knew. It's a wonderfully natural reaction, and the strange thing is that it works.

The first girl I knew from the Ton Son Nhut area started bargaining with me in Japanese slang. She thought it was English. She had picked it up from soldiers coming from Japan who wanted to make the same variety of deal that I did. The American thinks the message gets through because of his fluency in a foreign language. It is his happy ability to communicate his needs without any hangups. The Vietnamese finally learns through painful association what it really is that's being asked of him. Learning it, and being equally proud of being able to get the same thought across, the Vietnamese is eager to display his fluency too. He feels a sense of command; he has a new tool; he is using the same language the American uses for the same thought. In using it as English he reinforces the ecstasy of the American, who is now convinced that he has an instinct for the Vietnamese language. I've heard Cambodian whores jokingly swearing in Manila Spanish, expecting the customers to marvel at their English. Whatever it sounds like it is still a triumph over the language barrier, even though the communication has been established with words which each side thinks belong to the other but actually belong to neither.

In spite of the swirl of easily mixed slang to blend people, all the areas of Saigon have perfectly defined features. The Chinese sections, the Cambodian ghetto, the river people, the districts lying near the jungle—each has its distinct, ancient tone. Since Saigon has now become home for hundreds of thousands of refugees from the embattled areas throughout Vietnam it is amazing that these areas retain their personality.

Because I am more excessive than most it would be wrong to assume my experiences and pastimes were shared by all fellow Saigon Warriors to the same degree. Sometimes I wouldn't go to sleep for days when I was busily chasing the endless possibilities for excitement that Saigon offered. I can remember sometimes feeling like a feverish grandfather grabbing for a library of remarkable incidents to breathe life into my old age. I would continually get myself into an unbelievable situation just so I could get out of it and describe it later to my friends. By the end of my year there they had heard all the stories and lived many of them themselves. When we would get together, later, in a bar or at work, each would take his turn at astounding the others with personal accounts of how each day grew continually more remarkable than the days which had passed before.

Unlike the broadcast specialists who had come before me, I was to spend six months outside the sensory versatility of Saigon. But I had established my Vietnamese life style there within my first two weeks in the country.

I had had my twentieth birthday just a few days before I came to Saigon, and in the setting of this Army-occupied city I had planned to live out all the carnal images I'd found in numerous, lying, virile war novels. In my weeks before coming to Asia I had spent hours appreciating the truly beautiful Vietnamese women in the pages of *Time* and *Life*. I was assigned to a temporary hotel room for my first night in the city, with orders not to leave. But after the second day in the Reception Center I had made friends with one of the administrative sergeants and received all the information I needed to infiltrate the city's pleasure domes.

It was no great feat getting your ashes hauled in Saigon, but there were certain codes dictated by local customs and practice. The first Saigon attractions were the bars. Here the girls came in from the country to find a constant flow of attention and money in the charms of young America. If a girl made enough money she could afford to go to Hong Kong and have her breasts enlarged with silicone treatments (in fact the Saigon slang for these mutations is "Hong Kong"). With these new attractions she would make more money in the bar and after a few months she could go and get her eyes rounded. This kind of thing is, of course, very popular in the United States also and the American topless dancers are silicone fans, but more American women probably prefer the opposite abbreviating operation and nose-shortening rather than eye-rounding. However, many Vietnamese regard the practice as a national insult as well as outright Western wickedness. It's interesting that Vice President Nguyen Cao Ky's wife underwent this surgical route. Probably very few girls ever accumulated enough money to pay for these operations, but it was a great incentive to them and they saved and planned for that goal. The one thing they couldn't change was their overall proportions, and that was just as well as far as I was concerned. I found the delicate design of their bodies to be perhaps the most beautiful thing about the Vietnamese. If any soldier ever had sex fantasies about making love to twelve- or fourteen-year-old girls he could have felt fulfilled in Vietnam. In many cases they were perfectly developed women even by American standards, but two thirds the size. I remember at first I felt as if I was holding a child in my arms, and exotic children they were indeed. Sometimes they felt as if they might break, and still beneath the tender frame there was a spirit beyond any I have ever known.

After a bar girl had been fed enough "Saigon tea" (colored water at two dollars a shot) she might take you to a hotel or to her home, but there were no set rules for this. The most certain outlets for purely sexual energy were the whorehouses and steam baths. I have been told that fellatio in the Orient, particularly in Japan, is considered a medicinal and fairly accepted practice for sailors and fishermen in port. Because of the therapeutic tenor of this approach it was generally available in bath houses and was performed by female masseuses. The tradition spread to the port of Saigon, and by the time the American soldier had made it really big business it was referred to as a "steam job and blow bath." As I understand it, never having purchased the service myself, the once noble treatment had degenerated into a quick hustle, in which the massage consisted of a single stroke from head to waist, then the girl told you the massage was over and asked, "Hey GI, you fey two hundred piasters, I gib you number-one steam job."

Whorehouses were another thing altogether. About my third night out on the town I found myself in a very friendly little whorehouse near Cholon in the Chinese section. When I think about it now I can see myself as a very sincere, if horny, Peace Corps worker, who liked to do nothing more than sit and play with the Vietnamese and their way of life. Though of course there are thousands of variations in between, American soldiers for the most part fell into two categories of basic approach and feeling about the Vietnamese. Whichever it might be, the polarity of this mood was always accentuated in a whorehouse setting. Some would automatically talk to the girls and react to them as people. Many others went through what one imagines to be an ultimate human intimacy with a detachment born of not really believing these small, wiry Asians were any different from monkeys—certainly not the same as *Homo sapiens*. It reminded me very much about what many white Americans think about their black brothers and sisters. With both white and Negro GI's going to the whorehouses I tried to see whether or not there was any warm identification visible between the black GI's and the Vietnamese. But the Negroes were like the white GI's; some Negroes loved the Vietnamese, but most were contemptuous. I don't know how to estimate how many there were like myself, who loved everything the Vietnamese did, to the point of seeing greatness in place of simple human nature. I still think that was a wonderfully gratuitous bonus for being a soldier in Vietnam. I never saw any sign of what might be called vengeance involved with the ordinary GI's attitude with the ordinary Vietnamese. Their sometimes inhumane behavior was only a sad testament to their own fear and suspicion.

One particular evening in Cholon I got involved in an incident not long after I'd arrived at the whorehouse. In the back bedroom a scuffle broke out with a terrified GI who somehow thought the girls were Vietcong. He came bursting into the front room with a broken bottle, ripping down the mosquito netting around the various sleeping areas. I had no intention of getting involved with this nut, but I was standing between him and Mama-san, and the beer bottle he was wielding seemed to be intended for her. While I was in the process of yelling at the guy in English to be careful and calm down, he was mysteriously seized with panic and ran out the door. He was no doubt oblivious to my words, but the girls, who didn't understand what I was saying, thought I had saved the day and Mama-san's life as well. In the flood of their misplaced gratitude I was invited to move in. So I did.

All the GI's in Saigon were assigned to a certain hotel room, but there was no bed check, thus soldiers could maintain living quarters in another part of the city. As long as they kept a few clothes in their hotel room, bribed the Vietnamese maid to mess up the bed every morning, and reported to the billeting office, it appeared they lived at the hotel.

It only took a few days of living in my new home to make me realize I had to go elsewhere for sex. It became so much like living with a family that the idea of intercourse with my sisters was absurd. The Vietnamese have the greatest sense of humor in the Orient, and any possible romantic endeavor was laughed to death before single-minded eroticism had a chance to rear its stylized head. Jealousy was another factor forcing me to prowl away from home. In their childish way, my sisters' emotions wove in and out of their every thought and move. There was no damper of sophistication or affectation to color their spontaneity. From my nervous pubescent brushes with prostitutes in America and Europe I had come to imagine them as the most miserable people on earth—with perhaps the exception of aging homosexuals in the grips of psychological menopause. If I had been a better student of my father's novels I probably would have known better. Nevertheless the grimmer surfaces of reality that I had grown up with in New York City had left a dramatic impression on my thoughts about people. I had very little preparation for the innocence I now saw within this least innocent of professions. I enjoyed my life with these funny obvious people more than anything I had ever known. I quickly came to be treated with the contradicting privileges of equality and royalty. I had to share my brotherly affection, compassion, and playful devotion equally with all twelve girls, and in return I enjoyed the countless luxuries of respect, service, and comfort that the Oriental male has enjoyed since the beginning of civilization. Even though I learned to refrain from any hint of "incest," the thread of tiny jealousies still ran through my relationships with all the members of this family. I had a friend—I'll call him George—who ran into some fantastic difficulties in another whorehouse where he lived.

George was living with the Mama-san of a bar-whorehouse in the Cambodian ghetto of Saigon called Dachao. The Chez Jeannette, as it was called, was famous, and in Dachao George was king. In many ways Dachao was the strangest and wildest jungle of the city. There were a great many old and fine French homes scattered through the ghetto, but they were surrounded with shacks and alleys teeming with the life of the poor. George's girl friend was famous in her own right. She was very petite and dark and, as George would say, "a beautiful flowering fruit from the Cambodian jungle." Though small she had the heart of a tiger, and she ran the Chez Jeannette with devastating business sense. After George had won her through some uncommunicable charm of his, Simone started showing him the ropes of the business. Suddenly he was given the responsibility of breaking in all the virgins she enlisted out in the country. For many girls prostitution was without doubt a very attractive job. George once described the procedure many months later when we were both rotting on top of a little mountain, sitting out a twenty-two-day monsoon. From his description the part he played in the business was hardly enviable. Simone would bring the girls into a room and mount George on top of each new recruit. The instant he had penetrated and professionalized each piece Simone would shout "Enough!" and rip him off before he could do any more. Then she would send the girl to the bath and bring the next one in for George to anoint.

Though George had told the story and described the circumstances, apparently he didn't have a very practical appreciation of Simone's possessiveness. After we had left the mountain and returned to Saigon, George was indiscreet enough to try and sleep with Simone's bosomy cousin. Simone got wind of it somehow and broke down the door to the bedroom with a knife in her hand, but she quickly decided it would be rash to kill a relative and she stopped short of action. She made it clear that George was being spared, but only on special conditions. For security she saw to it that George found a GI boy friend for Simone's cousin to live with so that this wouldn't happen again. Despite their domestic problems Simone was a very powerful influence in the ghetto and George commanded tremendous respect and exercised great authority in Dachao. When it was decided I was to live in Cholon I took my model—with slight alterations—from him.

Within the city the magnifying glass of armed conflict, coupled with the organic ability of people to remain just exactly the way they were to begin with, sets off an explosion for the observer which is filled with vast clouds of images. The after-images become more and more laced with the absurd and the beautiful when a reality of cold, relentless, and impersonal war is re-superimposed on the daily actions of the men and the people who gave the war a reality in the first place.

People mold themselves and flow around and through the crevices of war—bending and flowing and adapting—so that they may remain themselves. They slowly change in order to remain the same. The interactions between people, though they may be in different settings and may use different tools, still remain unchangeable and eventually defeat war itself. It isn't really because war has made the people this way, or different, that is significant. Far stranger is that the actions, and the situations people find themselves in, are no more distorted or basically insane than at any other supposedly normal instant in time. It is the height of the absurdity that it turns out to be war itself that provides the lens which allows us to see it.

It is only with the contrast of possible death at any moment —no different from normal existence really—that we see for a moment, for a valueless time, empty of compare, and our egos reveal how very silly we are no matter what. In not being able to keep defensive logic in pace with the changes around us, we look over the torn edge and see what caricatures of ourselves we are. Almost one and indistinguishable. Almost. Here, in war, we can trace like a shadow the vague outline of how precarious is the image we hold of ourselves, particularly to the minds of these fleeting people around us. For once, the presupposed rocklike vantage point is seen as a self-conceived ledge, tied together with flimsy personalized information. It begins to crumble even faster as we catch ourselves looking at ourselves. It's fantastic to see the glint of that idea-ful, yet mindless self from which we as people presume to build life, change a land, reach out to hurt or embrace another person, decide the very fate of our children or a country.

The odd thing is that for the instant that all this is seen, everything is on the same level. No one thing we do is more or less strange than anything else. In the atmosphere of war people participate in their own humanity with extra speed and fervor. They seem to be running away from that same insight into themselves by packing their minds and time with more of the same interactions as if to prove the isolated picture wasn't true. The speed of life picks up and the picture becomes just one of so many frames in a film. In a city, in a war, humanity's breath is only more noisy because it's all happening so fast in one place.

In my year in Vietnam I traveled throughout the country for Armed Forces Radio and Television, but the actual duties of the job, though perhaps remarkable from the standpoint of other GI's, seem rather dull to relate. However, the freedom which the job allowed me in getting the most out of the country was remarkable. Twice I was anchored to the news department of upcountry TV sites for over two months each, but the rest of the time I was able to move around rather freely.

When I first arrived the curfew in Saigon was still midnight. I worked on a news shift from curfew until six in the morning. This meant the only time I didn't have free was when there was nothing much happening anyway. When I got off work in the early morning I would go back to my professional family and drink tea with them as they dislodged the GI's who had been house guests while I was at work. We would all go and spend the early morning down at the riverside big market (*cho lon*) that had given the section its Chinese name. Sometimes we ate right there. The market women cooked tasty morsels of fish and vegetables (on tiny *hibachi* stoves) doused with the famous *nuc mamh*—a fermented fish sauce. The stench of *nuc mamh* is overpowering for Americans. The girls showed me how to exhale when I first got the stuff near my mouth, so my nose wouldn't know. Actually the taste of it is quite mild and pleasant. After breakfast there we returned home and I usually slept until after the noon siesta. When I woke up I would start another day of what I considered to be educational debauchery.

Many of my friends at the radio station who had been in Vietnam for some months had apartments and bar girl friends who came home every night after work. As the connections between girl friends, and their cousins, and sisters, and nieces, grew, I found that I had about fifteen bar stops to make every night before I went to work, just to be properly sociable. I remember how ridiculous I would think it all was as I later dragged my exhausted mind through the last hours of my news shift, but the next evening I forgot about it and started the whole process over again.

As the war grew daily, Saigon became more a city of foreigners and refugees. The original population of Saigon was there all the time, but it became covered with the influx of humanity. The various personalities of the different groups arriving in Saigon became quite evident, and everyone you saw on the street could be placed in one of several categories. Within the Headquarters City the Allied soldiers consisted of Americans, Australians and New Zealanders, Koreans, Filipinos, and Thais, not to mention the South Vietnamese themselves. The Koreans brought nothing but contempt for the Vietnamese, whereas the Thais and Filipinos seemed to like them. The Australians, from the Vietnamese viewpoint, were exactly like Americans with their uninhibited forwardness. Many Australians and Americans became fast friends, as they did in World War II. I felt a tremendous affinity for the Australians myself.

Thousands of civilian engineers were imported to Vietnam by large contracting firms to build the American airbases and seaports needed to support the war. They were known by the initials of the companies they worked for— RMK, for example (Ramsey-McPherson-Knudsen). Most of these engineers were potbellied American construction workers who made about three hundred dollars a day pushing around Vietnamese coolies. They were paid tremendous bonuses by their employers to work in Vietnam, but there's no question that in 1966 most of these men had the safest and easiest jobs any middle-aged soldier of fortune could have hoped for.

There were many German and other merchant-marine sailors. Japanese and French businessmen came in and out of the city for one reason or another. But the most remarkable of all the transient groups was without doubt the American and world press. It was not so much that these people were remarkable as individuals, but rather that their mission had reached such giant proportions that reporting the war became almost as large as the operation of war itself. In the

MACV Information Office in Pleiku we had a cartoon on the wall depicting a squad deep in the jungle, calling in air support because they were surrounded by correspondents. This doesn't seem quite so funny now since their casualty rates, especially during the street fighting in Saigon, have risen so suddenly and tragically.

By mid-August the word had been released at the station that the first upcountry site for a TV van would be ready for installation by the beginning of September. The vans themselves were such self-contained units it really took only four men to run the TV station and keep it on the air. The actual installation was another matter. The vans were to arrive on the coast of Vietnam, from Sacramento, California, via the Philippines. The first site happened to be right on the coast, but the other six vans which followed had to be taken by convoy to their mountaintop positions throughout Vietnam. There was very little help available to construct these sites, so it was necessary to assign ten broadcast specialists to each position to build it up, as well as run and maintain the highly specialized equipment.

A list of the members of AFRT who were to make up the first TV team in the field was posted, and my name was on it. I had been in Saigon a little over two months, and now it seemed as if I was suddenly being torn away from the best home and life I had ever had. The news of my move to the solitude of the field came to me with more alarm than my draft orders. Like a spring vacation from my youth the days had flown by filled with fast and furious activity. Our unit was still very small at this time (about twenty-three men), and some of the names listed were technically expendable to the Saigon operation and some were not. We were still operating out of the basement of a hotel, but construction was already underway for a huge radio-and-television complex in Saigon in addition to the upcountry sites we would install. Since we were all PIO's there was much more room for politicking to try and get out of being sent away than there is in the infantry. But since many more vans were coming and it was likely that everyone in AFRT would see duty in the field, the orders were frozen and the day finally came for us to leave for Qui Nhon, on the coast of the central highlands.

Armed Forces Radio and Television, Detachment Number One, left Saigon on the first of September, and we spent a month getting ready to go on the air. The engineers went to work setting up the electronic end of the operation, working out the bugs in the new experimental equipment. Though the van was only the size of a regular truck van, the tiny station had a live news booth and facilities to broadcast a continuous stream of normal TV programming complete with propaganda commercials. I was in charge of the news department—news would be relayed to me by teletype from Saigon all day long—but when we arrived at the site my evening performances were a long way off. First, living and working quarters, in the form of a large Quonset hut and numerous tents, had to be erected. Defensive positions and bunkers had to be built. We spent far more time filling sandbags than polishing our skills in broadcasting. At that time Qui Nhon was a relatively safe area and the mountains were full of Korean soldiers. Qui Nhon happened to be Ho Chi Minh's birthplace, however, and the North Vietnamese were forever vowing to capture the city in honor of their leader.

I managed to go back to Saigon once in a while to pick up equipment for the unit, but most of the time we were all very much there on the mountaintop for twenty-four hours of every day. George and I, who had been exiled together, spent hours bemoaning our plight, late at night in our tent. Occasionally I could leave for a few hours to go into the village below and try to rebuild my city-style life with the country people. These moments are the finest part of my memories of the entire Qui Nhon experience. I always felt very light, as if my body didn't exist, when I escaped the military, and my soldier-self, through watching these people. Because of their small stature their houses seem tiny to a Westerner, and the

whole effect is quite Gulliver-producing even for a person
of medium height like myself. I know that everything these
simple people were doing was not in itself extraordinary, but
because of their exceptional physical grace and symmetry,
their easy and pleasant manners, it was infinitely satisfying
to be with them.

I was miserable a great deal of the time I spent away from
Saigon, and because of this most of my recollections of Army
duties in Qui Nhon have melted away. However, there was
one morning ritual which will remain in my memory always.
Latrine duty in the upcountry field positions was often as
new to some of the old soldiers as it was to the draftees. Many
of the men who had fought in Europe had moved fairly
quickly, camping in fields and frequently bivouacked in
some established dwelling. In Vietnam the military most
often found itself holding a position for weeks or months.
The practice of burning shit may have started in Korea, but
it came into its heyday in Vietnam. The method involved
fifty-gallon oil drums which were cut in half to make two
huge buckets. These buckets were placed under the appropriate openings in a two-hole outhouse, to receive the fruits
of military field cooking. A large pit was dug about sixty feet
from the outhouse, and it was our unit's detail to drag the
buckets from the outhouse in the morning, pour the contents
into the pit, and then set fire to it by covering the mixture
with Diesel fuel.

One morning when it happened to be my turn to conduct
this operation I had great difficulty in whipping up the
flames. I'll never complain about a balky fireplace or a smoky
campfire again. The problem seemed insurmountable. First
of all there was no light whatever, except for the feeble glim-
mer of the burning toilet-paper torch I kept relighting in my
hands to use as an igniter. This duty, by some never-to-be-
questioned Army regulation, had to take place before breakfast, which was at six thirty a.m. One of my friends used to
complain sarcastically to our sergeant, saying it should be
done after breakfast because the detail made him so hungry.

I had a short pole with which to stir up the shit in order that all of it might be exposed to the burning fuel, which tended to stay on the top. The upper surface would become crusted over from the heat, like a casserole, but when it was stirred, the bubbling fresh underlayer would invariably put the rest of the flame out. This same friend had given me a large lighter with the indignant words "I am a Broadcast Specialist" embossed on the case, to be used especially for this task, but it wouldn't do the job that morning because this particular mix I was coping with seemed soggier than usual. Ten times I had it burning only to see the flames flutter out. Cursing and trying not to splash it all over me (which was of course impossible to avoid), I poled and stirred the shit like some deviant gondolier, but all to no avail. After about twenty frustrating minutes of this, the sentry came over to see what was going on and we were both struck with a tremendous idea. The reason Diesel fuel was used was that it burned a long time, but because of this quality it was also hard to light. We poured more Diesel fuel onto the mass, and this time we also poured about ten gallons of high-test gasoline. I stirred it all up, being careful to leave a thick layer of pure gas on top, and stood back. The sentry raised his weapon and fired a magazine of tracers into the hole, exploding the shit, which immediately started to roar into flames. Within moments everyone was running around in the dark, screaming and yelling, trying to figure out why the outhouse was under attack. It was getting light, and a thick brownish-yellow pall of smoke covered and hung about our mountaintop. The addition of the gasoline had seriously altered the whole chemistry, and the smoke from that fire was of a special nature, leaving everything it came into contact with smelling of broiled shit. I took a cold shower out of my helmet and went to breakfast.

Not long after we went on the air in mid-October, and Detachment Number Two was ensconced on their mountain near Da Nang, our Saigon office was compiling the list of names for the unit which would man Detachment Number Three. It was to be the first "combat television van," because transmission purposes demanded it be isolated on a small mountain near the Cambodian border about nine miles from Pleiku. The detachment would be easy prey for Viet Cong mortar attack because the red light on top of the sixty-foot TV antenna would provide an excellent target. The Saigon office preferred to ask for volunteers for this post rather than make an arbitrary list. When news of this reached me I told my colonel I would build a TV station in Hanoi for him if I could leave Qui Nhon and be assured of spending my last three months of duty in Saigon after the job was done. Since the construction of the site was the hard part, and he would need me later for the new ground station in Saigon after the job was done, he agreed, and I was removed from Qui Nhon and sent back to Saigon to wait for the formation and departure of Detachment Number Three for Pleiku. It was even considered valuable that I be the guiding member of the new team, because at that time I was the only soldier in AFRT who had already had experience setting up a van. I marvel now at the wisdom involved in sending ten radio and television announcers, with little or no combat experience, to a secluded mountaintop which was almost like a road stop on the Ho Chi Minh Trail.

Since I knew what my orders were concerning the new detachment I had a friend sign in at the office for me when I arrived in Saigon and went straight to a Vietnamese friend's apartment. As I rode from the air base into the city toward my first real shower in over two months the late morning sun warmed me in the open taxi and my joy was unbounded. We made our way slowly, over the river, pushing through crowds of these wonderful people I had come to love. I felt that I had never been so happy in my life. Maybe it was all founded on banal and normal reaction, common to any soldier coming to a city after the field. But I felt a very special sense of freedom from myself, as if I were carried on a teeming Möbius strip of exposure, involved and yet free. It was a mystery.

When I arrived at the apartment my friend wasn't home. I put away my rifle and pistol, climbed out of my jungle fatigues, lit a pipeful of marijuana. In moments I was sitting on the floor of the hot shower, protecting the fire in my pipe with cupped hands. Though George and I had spent endless hours in daydreams, fantasizing about what we liked to do best in Saigon, and where we would be if we could be there suddenly by magic, I had no idea right away about what to do. It was a classic momentary lapse, and the next five days and nights were spent in saying hello to all my friends and their endless families. It wasn't until a week had passed from my arrival in Saigon that I finally made an appearance at the office, and then only to pick up my mail. Most of the people at the station thought I was still in Qui Nhon, and it wasn't my plan to attract their attention to my holidays by hanging around the studios. The word at the station was that Detachment Number Three wouldn't be leaving for Pleiku for some time yet, because the van had been lost in the paperwork somewhere between the Philippines and Vietnam. A million-dollar piece of equipment as big as a moving van had been misplaced. After saying hello to a few friends at the office I retreated back into the city.

After the field Saigon glittered with even more delight for me. But as my vacation from work was extended because of more and more delays, the newness of my activities began to fade. Long before I had ever been drafted into the Army I tended to impose a certain routine on my day-to-day surroundings, whatever they might be, through the pattern of after-work or after-school strolls. Saigon was a complicated Oriental box of possibilities, but in time, the routine met the challenge by simply becoming complicated itself. As I took on a gradual distaste for the mindlessness of my mechanical appetite I began to notice more and more the absurdities all around me in the city where war had become big business.

When I first arrived in Saigon, in 1966, I had been sent to the field on a few occasions to make tapes and get stories firsthand from units out on operations, and in actual combat, but that was only for one or two days at a time. When I returned from Qui Nhon I became much more sensitive to the decadence at the core of the cause which all those people were dying for. Since I spent what seemed like a great deal of time almost in a bunker one day and in a night club the next, the contradictions grew more and more unbearable. Unbearable isn't the correct word, since I managed to bear up sufficiently to make it to the bars every night with very little emotional disturbance. Finally, though, in some concession to an apparent absurdity or contradiction that I wouldn't contain, I began going out to the air base, where I was quickly accepted as a volunteer gunner on the "dust-off" and evacuation helicopters which flew out by the hundreds every day on impromptu missions. After doing this about five times I learned to isolate the sound of bullets ripping through a helicopter, and some very close shaves made me decide to give up my career as volunteer gunner. My problems of conscience continued. My short stint in the choppers exposed me to more dead and maimed human beings than I could ever have imagined at one time. I didn't feel any political debt, but I did feel I owed something for the fear and the absolute horror that was happening and being experienced by so many people who would never see a bar or a bed or a laugh again. How could this all be permitted beyond the walls of my pleasure garden? How could the champagne whimsy of Washington and Saigon ever justify the endless hours of despair for the fighting and the dying, hours that I and so many others were spending simultaneously in comparative bliss?

By December the days were passing into themselves. Each one seemed to vanish into the one before; it was as if there was some kind of instant tropical decay at work rather than the spool of history. It seems to be peculiar to the strange life of a city in wartime. To the men in the field who lived and functioned so much of the time as soldiers there is an automatic adjustment to this continuous fabric of time. Even with firefights in and around the city, Saigon still remained essentially ornamental, if not parasitic, in a way quite separate from the actual war of the field. Zigzagging between the soldier's reality and the civilian's reality, even though you do it every day, creates a special kind of unreal transiency.

On one particular day, I checked in at the office briefly in the early evening, and then went to the roof of the nearest enlisted men's hotel to get some cheap drinks at the bar. My ability to love my life in Saigon was slowly degenerating into a general dismay about the war, but I was still caught up in a pattern of what felt like waking slumber which carried me through the evenings. In comparison the lives of my friends in the States seemed unbelievably dull, though I knew my pattern to be equally repetitious and aimless. From the roof-top bar I saw flares shoot up in the early twilight sky over Ton Son Nhut air base. Whatever meaning it may have had for the defenders of the base, for me it was the signal that another night had begun. Another night, like all the others, with the same differences.

Of the thousands of bars that infest Saigon I had never been in the Flowers before. I had been told that the girls there were beautiful, hard, detached in their active way, and expensive. With this in mind I had always avoided it as something to save for a night when I felt especially good. My girl friend at the Liz Bar had gone to Dalat for the month-long funeral of her grandmother. It was payday and I decided to see what the Flowers was all about.

The Flowers had a long, dark bar which seemed to be better decorated than the usual Saigon not-so-tender trap. The bar obviously made a great deal of money because of its location on Tu Do street, the Broadway of Saigon. On payday, Tu Do street, which is only about eight blocks long, pulled in several hundred thousand dollars from the soldiers stationed in Saigon and those from upcountry who were sent down to the big city for rest and recuperation. Protection money to both the National Police and the Viet Cong accounted for most of that money, however, and the bar owners rarely got really rich.

When I walked in a girl grabbed me with a robotlike enthusiasm and pulled me into a booth off to the side of the main bar area. With the usual ritual of introduction thus taken care of, she ordered me a beer, then finally turned to look at her prize. I heard a low laugh, and as the immediate darkness grew light to my eyes, I saw who she was. It was Kim Tchi, the sister of plain Tchi; Tchi had been living with an Army friend of mine, Rick. Through Rick I had met Kim Tchi before, on several occasions. I had always marveled at the girl, but she had been swallowed up into Oriental secrecy when her sister had run off from Rick a few months earlier. The sister had taken with her all that was in his apartment and most of Rick's confidence in humanity as well.

Rick had been living with Tchi for well over a year. He had been stationed upcountry with the First Air Cavalry and had met Tchi on a three-day pass to Saigon. When he was through with his year in the infantry he extended his hitch, working as a newswriter for the radio-television station in order to get an additional six months in Vietnam, and moved with Tchi into an apartment near the Saigon Pagoda. When I met him he had extended for another year. His one goal was to spend his entire enlistment in the Army living in domestic bliss in the middle of a war. One night Rick came home to find that his television, motorcycle, tape recorder, clothes, and everything else he owned had all disappeared. Not the least of these losses was Tchi herself. When this happened all the girls who knew Tchi suddenly didn't remember her name. Tchi's sister, Kim Tchi, had been working in a bar on Hai Ba Trong street, but the night after the great vacuum developed in Rick's material and romantic life she too disappeared and no one would say where she had gone.

Several months earlier Rick had introduced me to Kim Tchi and had told me she was looking for a boy friend who didn't fit the average mold. In the mind of every GI this was each of us. Both the girls were wonderfully insane, though, and perhaps it did take a different sort of soldier to catch on to their sense of humor. This sense of humor was such that the disappearance of both girls might well have been one big joke they were content to laugh over with each other. Now, here was Kim Tchi again, in all her callous splendor.

To this day, I remember Kim Tchi as the most sensual woman I have ever met. She had a fantastically deep voice for a Vietnamese and a steady, sure way about her that was more than disquieting. She spoke English quite well and with an inflection that made her sound like an Oriental Marlene Dietrich. Kim Tchi had been living with a wealthy American RMK engineer for over two years, but when he wanted to marry her it got in the way of her fun, whatever that was, and she left him the same way Tchi left Rick.

There was a good deal of French blood in Kim Tchi. Certainly she showed it more than her sister did. Her long, apparently black hair had myriad glints of chestnut in it, which hypnotized me as it reflected the bar lights. She was truly beautiful, with rounder eyes than Keane ever dreamed of. In contrast to supple beauty her face was etched with what might have been whiskey lines. My romantic young mind attributed them to the life of constant exposure to anything and everything, and I enjoyed the idea that it was this she loved. She never really reacted to much other than herself, but in spite of this attitude of self-concerned coldness, her mouth was always marked with a dry smile. With the exception of her sister, Kim Tchi laughed more than any other girl in Southeast Asia. But then, in this war in Saigon she had a lot to laugh about. Everything was a joke, even if a cruel one, to be made more serious by something that was even more amusing.

In the bar where she had been active before, the Biloxi, I once saw her working over a GI as only she could. At first, from the way she behaved, I thought she was living with him as well as with the RMK engineer. Her method was really something to see. By not seeming to care about a hustle she

got more Saigon tea than any girl in the bar. She was destroy-
ing this guy's mind and digesting his pay like a voracious
Venus flytrap when suddenly two Koreans rushed into the
bar, knocked the soldier off his stool, and stabbed him several
times as he lay on the floor. They were gone in an instant. It
might have been a personal thing, or they might have been
paid by someone else to do it. The soldier died quickly in the
sawdust. Watching all this, without a blink, Kim Tchi turned
to the stunned soldier sitting on her right and said, "My
boy friend number-ten GI, he die and fini me. You buy me
Saigon tea?" Exciting herself with her ability to carry this
off, she suddenly broke into uncontrollable laughter. (In
Saigon slang, people are rated from one to ten, one being the
finest and ten the worst.) When her shrieks of delight with
herself had died down she slapped the bar with her purse to
get business going again as the soldier next to her ran after
the MP's.

Kim Tchi and I had always gotten along well. I knew her
for the spontaneous monster she was and I never disapproved.
She would often do her worst to shake me up, but I would
always encourage her to be even more monstrous and stop the
trend before it gathered momentum. In the Biloxi, while I
was waiting for it to close, I sometimes pointed out GI's at the
door whom I thought she could really go to work on. Whatever affection there was between us was due to my not messing
with her work or the way she lived by Putting an American
Value on it all. I knew that if I too died right there, she
would perhaps kiss my cold mouth as she went through my
pockets looking for whatever I might have left behind. She
knew that I knew this and so everything was all right. We
were good friends when we thought about it, but there was
rarely time for that. There was time now to know that I had
genuinely missed her ever since she had disappeared from
the other bar.

When she saw who I was, sitting on the dark side of the
booth at the Flowers, and I saw her, there wasn't the slightest
change of expression on her perpetually smiling face, as she

said, "John, I love you, give me a thousand piasters." I gave her the ten dollars, a challenge without any questions. She handed it over to another girl behind the bar and the money was never mentioned again. The only way to tell anything had taken place between us was from the increased intensity of the magnificent sneering smile which seemed to flicker across her mouth.

I spent most of the night drinking more and more beer as she listed the doleful reasons why her sister had been forced to leave Rick. I told her I didn't believe a word she said, adding that was as it should be, but still I asked her to continue. She was very rarely frustrated in just this manner, but she enjoyed it when it did happen.

Because it was payday the bar became very crowded around eleven o'clock. A large Australian soldier came stumbling in, waving a lot of money. I knew what was coming. In a second Kim Tchi was gone from my booth. It was instantly clear that my imagined intimate reunion with her later that night was not going to take place. I couldn't and wouldn't outdo this. If she wanted money, even if it was just to ask for it, I would donate, but otherwise I never paid for anything but her drinks. I indulged myself, thinking my style made me different from others.

My expectant delight at seeing Kim Tchi again quickly turned into a depressed stupor. The strong Vietnamese beer hit me hard when she departed, and as I pondered this feeling of heaviness I realized just how interested in a girl, any girl, I had become.

As curfew drew near at midnight the Flowers began to close up fast. The girls were changing their clothes and the bar boys came around collecting the various checks, which indicated by code number how many Saigon teas the girls with the corresponding numbers had promoted. The GI's were filtering out of the bar, with girls or alone, in a hurry to get back to their hotels or just off the street by curfew. On the way out Kim Tchi and her new friend passed by me. As usual, everything was well in control for her. For a brief moment

Kim Tchi distracted the Australian's attention by pointing to the ceiling, talking about the last grenade that had been tossed into the bar. As he gazed up at the scars in the plaster she reached over and pinched me hard on the inside of my thigh. She giggled for a second as she glided past my chair and beyond my aspirations. She was chattering about the "number-ten VC" who had thrown the grenade as she vanished without the slightest change in her unshakable poise.

Outside the streets were wet from an early-evening rain. A drunken soldier had passed out in the street and the children were dancing up and down, fooling with sticks in the vomit surrounding his head, while he was oblivious to their natural and somehow unmalicious glee in tormenting him. Soon the Allied MP's would come by to sweep him up.

The air was filled with the noise of revving motorcycles and scooters. The owners were selling rides back to the air base and to the hotels, beating the taxis out of their higher fares. The curfew songs of Saigon rang through the streets.

"Hey GI, you want number-one girl? She bery young . . . she boom-boom number one."

"Hey, you want two number-one girls? You no like, you no hap fey!"——you don't have to pay.

"Hey, you want dream number-one? Want buy opium? Marijuana? Buy girl too, smoke make boom-boom number-one. Me no sao, no lie GI."

"Hey, you want cherry girl? Number-one girl, still hap cherry. I show you picture. She dep hoa, she very byoo-tee-fu, yes?"

"Hey GI, you want change money? I gib you beaucoup Vietnamese money for green . . . me number-one prend of beaucoup GI."

"Hey, where you go? Ton Son Nhut? I gib you number-one ride. We go tout suite. Beaucoup cheap."

"Hey you, you number-one GI, beaucoup handsome. I hap number-one girl, she do everything you like, for sur . . . me no sao, for sur, I no lie you."

With my dejection setting in on top of the beer, and the

small amount of marijuana I had smoked earlier, I decided that a number-six girl would do just fine to help me forget about Kim Tchi. At least it would do until the next night. I piled into the nearest cyclo, a sort of pedal-driven rickshaw, and gave the boy my order by number. It came out something like this: "You no sao me . . . go gib take me number-six girl, tout suite, OK?" The cyclo-boy looked at me enterprisingly and said, "Shaigong hap all number-ten girl, beaucoup sick all time, you get sick too. You get beaucoup dao hoa, maybe hap die. I show you number-one girl in Gia Dinh. You know Gia Dinh? Maybe ten minute. You hap number-one girl . . . me no sao you, me no lie. I show you number-one girl for sur. Girl I show you boom-boom number-one and she no sick, she no dao hoa like Shaigong girl who boom-boom too many GI—she number-one, she boom-boom ti-ti, not beaucoup like Shaigong girl, she number-one for sur!"

Though the numbers game amused me I knew he didn't really understand the precise mood I was expressing with my preference that moment for a number-six girl. He figured in terms of number-one and number-ten, very polarized. So I said, "OK, you di-di . . . soon hap curfew, you no go tout suite maybe MP do me number-ten and fini me. Now di-di mao, we go, OK?" He told me he was my "number-one prend for sur" and we took off.

We started out of the city in the direction of the air base at Ton Son Nhut, my cyclo-boy pedaling like mad to impress me with his earnestness in taking care of my sexual problems. After a few minutes I began to feel a bit nervous about his intentions because of his evasiveness about just exactly where he was taking me. The "ten-minute ride" seemed more like an hour. The air base was quite a way out of the city, and when we reached it we didn't stop. We skirted around its farthest edge, coming almost to the edge of the jungle in Gia Dinh province. I began to regret I hadn't brought my automatic; on other occasions I had also failed to have it when it looked like I might need it. In itself, my mental picture of the gun lying ineffectually in my dresser drawer was a mild signal for me that this was going to be an eventful night. My alcoholic courage was up, though, and I knew that turning around to go back at this late hour was sure to mean running into the MP's.

During this period the Viet Cong were constantly infiltrating the air base, blowing up ammunition pads when they could. Several Air Force sentries and their dogs had been killed. About twelve VC had been shot on the perimeter of the field during the previous two days. It was two months before Operation Cedar Falls was to pacify the area known as the Iron Triangle, which surrounded Saigon with an estimated five Viet Cong battalions. The Viet Cong had not just recently moved in. They had been there for nine years as a military group and the cadre of these units had lived there since the Japanese occupied Vietnam thirty years earlier. Huge flares hung in the sky over Ton Son Nhut like floating chandeliers, and the small-arms fire got louder and louder as we circled the base and went farther out on the "tout suite" ride. In retaliation to my nervous system I lit my pipe. The cyclo-boy giggled as he smelled the marijuana smoke.

After we had gone well over two miles past the river into Gia Dinh, my driver started down several alleys which were wide enough for a couple of motorcyclists to pass each other. I had done some pretty crazy things in daylight, like riding in a jeep for miles on a mined road, but I had never been this far out of the city by myself at night. Finally we arrived at a two-story house set in a labyrinth of narrow streets. The cyclo-boy dismounted and gestured at me grinningly. We went inside.

A slim middle-aged Chinese man greeted me as if he'd been expecting me. Prices were agreed on for the ride and the girl. Cyclo-boys were roving pimps, and this one may have had some tie-in with the Flowers bar. The boys received a cut from the house owners for any GI they could bring out to do business.

It was a huge room for a Vietnamese house. The only houses of this size I had been in were all sectioned off with curtains and straw mattresses so that several girls could work in the same room. I began to wonder if it really was a whorehouse. There was only one bed in the corner of this big room, and it was the only piece of furniture. The bed was draped from above with a cascade of mosquito netting; there was a single Army blanket and another drop curtain for privacy. After the boy made a joke to the Papa-san about my pipe, they both left and a girl entered from a door in the back of the room.

The girl introduced herself as Mai. She was very dark-complexioned and dressed in horrible pink pajamas. Her large, black, misshapen nipples, which must have known many a child's toothless gums, danced behind her pajama top like a pair of big black thumbs. I asked her if she was Cambodian. She looked a little surprised, then she smiled and agreed she was. She told me how she had crossed the border into Vietnam with her parents through the jungles because they had heard there was much money in Vietnam. All the GI's were "beaucoup rich." She said her parents had been killed near the border by "beaucoup number-ten big bombs" (probably a B-52 raid) but nevertheless she had finished the pilgrimage to Saigon alone. As the conversation continued we got into bed. I enjoyed carrying on these ethnic pseudo-psychological discussions in my street Vietnamese, impressing the poor people with my sordid fluency. Because of her Cambodian dialect we got much more accomplished in sordid English, which she was quite fluent in.

After she lit some incense to keep the insects away I began to hear muffled voices coming from the outer entranceway. When Mai heard them she became extremely nervous. I inquired what was wrong but she wouldn't tell me at first. I kissed her. She brushed it off like a mosquito bite and said I had better hurry up and get on with the business at hand. Before I could immediately assert my libido she asked me where my wallet was. When I gave it to her she listened for a moment to the whispers out in front and then quickly hid it behind a brick in the wall. I was about to consummate the

night's transaction when she suddenly stopped everything
and told me I was in real trouble.

"Cyclo-boy who take you here he number-ten boy. He talks
with beaucoup prends outside. They want cacadow you . . .
cut you neck . . . fini money, fini you. Here, take back money.
You di-di now. Go way fast. I gib you back money. You still
baby-san, you no stay here. Cyclo-boy and cowboys do you
number-ten. They fini you for sur, me no sao you . . . you di-
di mao now."

I asked her how many there were, and she held up eight
fingers, before her widening black eyes. Within two seconds
I was cold sober. It took all the bluffing I could muster to
fight down the growing panic that was beginning to rise up
and choke me. To compensate for my fear the only way out
I could see was to display put-on confidence and anger. These
boys weren't Viet Cong; they were what the Vietnamese
called "cowboys." For the most part they are young hoods
and draft dodgers who spend their time mugging GI's and
stealing motorcycles. Mai returned my wallet and I dressed
quickly right in bed. Then to overemphasize my control of
the situation I crossed the room and kicked down the flimsy
door to the entranceway. Eight men, or boys, were sitting on
the earthen floor in a quiet but heated discussion. They froze
with the noise and surprise of the door collapsing in front of
them. I started yelling at the top of my lungs that I was an
American MP with many friends nearby. I stomped back and
forth, screaming at them. I picked up two of the lightest ones,
threw them against the wall, and continued to shout that I
had paid my money, I wanted peace, I wanted to be alone.
I'm sure they didn't understand many of the things I was saying, but the more intoxicated I became with my own sense
of reckless power, added to the gnawing fear inside me, the
more effective I became at intimidating them. I kicked each
one of them individually out of the house and into the street
and yelled after them that they would go to jail at the hands
of my "friends" if they came back. When I slammed the door
shut I collapsed on the floor, bathed in my triumph, the

adrenalin shaking my body apart. After a few minutes I had control of my muscles; I went back to bed and without saying a word I made love to Mai and fell asleep with relief.

It must have been two hours later when I woke up just in time to see three of the "cowboys" through the mosquito netting, jumping toward the bed with clubs. The Vietnamese are small-boned in the first place, and the lack of calcium in their diet makes their bones break easily. As I kicked the first one in the chest I could feel the delicate ribs snap. He let out a scream and the other two ran out the door as I tried to untangle myself from the now wet curtain around the bed. When the scream of the boy woke Mai up she had pissed all over everything. I got loose, kicked the kid at my feet a few more times, and ran out the door naked after the others. I could hear the clapping of their sandals as they disappeared down the alley. When I came back in the room the broken boy was gone and so was Mai.

As I was getting dressed I heard a rustling at the window, so I turned off the lights. After a few seconds the lights mysteriously went on again. This thing was turning into a Vincent Price horror show with each new development. I didn't want to be seen from the street, but every time I turned the lights off someone upstairs in the top of the house turned them back on again. I knocked out all the light bulbs in the room and climbed the ladder-stairs to the top of the house, where I found a man and his wife and child lying down in the corner of a room exactly like the one downstairs. This man, like the Chinese Papa-san, seemed to have expected me; he smiled, then gave a nervous little laugh. I picked him up and shoved him down the ladder. Carrying the woman and the little boy with me, I broke all the light fixtures on that floor as well. I put the three of them out in the alley and returned to the room where I'd been sleeping with Mai. After bolting the door I searched for something to use as a weapon. I was stranded alone in the dark house near the jungle and there was no question I would have to wait until dawn before I dared try to get back to Saigon.

All this time I had been shouting and bellowing to sound as crazed and dangerous as possible. The fear that came welling up in me only went away in fractional heartbeats as the false brutality became strong enough in me to convince me it wasn't false at all. To keep from being only the complete object of this macabre melodrama I *had* to be the avenger. Everything became very quiet then. In the distance I could hear faint machine-gun fire coming from the air base. A rat ran tinkling through the broken glass in the dark.

After a while, being all alone in the big empty room started to bother me. I crept outside into the alley, and stumbled over something. It was the club the first boy had dropped when he crawled away. I picked it up, kept moving slowly, and found a little niche in the wall farther down the alley. I crouched there, ready to wait until morning. Vietnamese alleys are like jungle paths made of stone. Wooden balconies hang on the sides of the houses over the narrow streets, suggesting the forest canopy. The alleys and the streets wind around and around only to meet themselves or another that looks like the first so much that it might as well be the one you just turned from. More flares descended slowly over Ton Son Nhut. As they dropped, making the sky black against their brilliance, the corresponding shadows in the alley rose in eerie complement to their descent. Suddenly there was a huge explosion that lit the sky completely with the white, then yellow, then orange of a twentieth-century hell. An ammunition pad had been hit. Air strikes started coming in on the perimeter of the base to "harass and interdict" however many infiltrators might be lurking there. It was nothing new. This sort of thing happened every night. In a duality that was getting harder for me to accept, Saigon Warriors, sometimes also called Remington Rand's Raiders, could watch the war every night, sipping gin or smoking marijuana on the rooftop bars of all the hotels in Saigon. How insane that people should be fighting and dying and at the same time provide a cordite-flavored stage show for a military cocktail crowd while Filipino rock-and-roll singers at the bar produced the musical background. The drums and cymbals would sometimes sizzle with the concussion of a nearby explosion.

Helicopter gunships began to strafe the jungle about half a mile from me, and the old DC-3 "Gooney Birds," with their incredible series of multibarreled electric Gatling machine guns mounted along the sides, were everywhere. They re-created something very like the fountains of Versailles with their tracer bullets that spiraled their slow red trails thousands of feet down to the earth. Those beautiful fountains could chop down a football field's worth of jungle in a second's burst from the pilot's trigger. At least this time I was kneeling, tiny, afraid in an alley, far from the sound of jingling ice cubes and electric guitars. Somehow it seemed more fitting to be watching the show from the dark alley.

The holocaust went on beyond and over my head, and then I heard soft footsteps coming down on the stones of the alley. The cowboys were coming back, and it sounded like all of them. I peeked out and watched the line they made winding down the street toward the house. I clenched the club I had picked up, which was a two-by-four with a groove for a hand-hold carved out of it. I waited for the first one in line to come up to where I was hiding. In a file they looked like any squad coming down a trail.

When the first one crept past where I was crouching I jumped out of my hole, swinging the club as hard as I could at his head. There was a crunching noise as his skull smashed. He dropped without a sound.

At first the others didn't realize what had happened, and neither did I really. When the image of the boy quietly slumped at my feet was registered in my brain, I ran at the others swinging my club erratically, screaming and screaming and screaming and screaming. Like cats they turned and ran before I could hit anyone else. I ran after them for a few feet and then dropped to the ground myself, suddenly exhausted. I tried not to understand in any sane symbols what had just happened. I didn't want to look at the almost decapitated boy lying in the alley. As I gazed past the lump of the body I didn't want to see, I caught the reflection of a flare in the blood covering the dirt and stones. The light was clearly captured in the pool and the flare looked as if it were rising up at me out of the ground. My hand could still feel the easy crunch that had been telegraphed up the stick to my hands, to my heart and in a circle to the memory of it all again and again and again.

I moved farther down the alley in the direction they had fled and found another doorway to wait out the rest of the night. They didn't come back. Things quieted down at the air base toward dawn. As soon as the sun came up and curfew was over I walked across the river. It was Sunday morning. The children of Saigon were already up, running and yelling. Soon they would find the body of the boy I had left. I could picture them singing and throwing stones at it. A new treasure left in the street to be prodded and to make them feel important. It would be something interesting to play with and discuss before anyone else had found anything in the city's morning. The women would presently come out and point and gossip and jabber about noises they had heard in the night, noises other than the bombs, which had become ordinary night sounds for them. Perhaps by noon the boy would be dragged away.

It becomes more and more difficult to tie up the fragments of my thoughts at this time to paint a logical progression toward a political reawakening that my mind now holds to for its moral comfort. This is mainly because the direction of logic is no direction at all. A great deal of my time had been spent avoiding any confrontation with the war as a subject of right and wrong. Of course I had a lot to say on the subject, but that too was a way of not thinking about it too much. The object seemed to be one of keeping both my mind and body alive with the least amount of emotional turmoil.

When I saw the armed military relocation of hundreds of thousands of people away from their lands, their families, and the sacred graves of their ancestors, I saw it as the skillful evacuation to "safety" of an entire village, accomplished through a masterpiece of logistical and political planning. After all, that peasant woman's tears would probably stop when she saw the American twentieth century with its porcelain bathrooms and bright neon, when she saw that a new democracy was now certain one day when she would be free from the oppression of her Viet Cong brother and her Viet Cong son. With this in mind it didn't seem important that her ancient city or village had been leveled after she was moved to protect her from her home. And if it was done with the use of napalm, or antipersonnel fragmentation bomblets —well, after all, we used them in Korea and nobody made a stink. Even if it was done with information acquired from the interrogation of Viet Cong prisoners by the Republic's soldiers—the method was to push them sequentially out of American helicopters hovering at about one thousand feet, either before or after interrogation as the case might be—if this was true, and certainly it couldn't be true, but if it was . . . well, war was just plain hell, it had never been any good anyway, and still, it was better than what the Viet Cong probably did with their prisoners.

Suffice it to say that anything I saw, I saw the way I wanted to see it. The hammer of national policy always hit the nail of justified morality on the head for what I believed—and why not? It was my hammer, and my nail, and I was doing all the swinging. I hadn't been taught to do this by an older generation's innocent heroism in previous wars. I was trying to modify their much more spontaneous and genuine ideals to fit my situation. In a pinch for logic it was easier that way. But while their motivations were indicative of their patriotism, and their generation, and the natural result of their era and conflicts, I began to feel increasingly that I hadn't come by them honestly.

My parents lived through World War II secure in feeling the United States was at war for a just cause. Then the philosophy that those who will not learn from history are condemned to repeat it suggested that steps would be taken so that never again would the United States wait to be attacked. We would become the policemen of the world, even if reluctantly, filling in all the vacuums left by the crumbling European overseas empires. But history is not something outside ourselves that we can judge and maneuver as if it were some external object. We make our history as we are our history. In reacting against its lessons we make more of the same. We carry history within us. As a Zen saying puts it, "If the dunce who was looking for fire, by the light of a lantern, understood what fire was, he could have cooked his rice much sooner." Americans were isolationists before World War II, and our statesmen saw the folly of that course. But by trying desperately to prevent that attitude from being repeated our statesmen have steered us into a position where we really are piteously isolated. My generation grew up entirely within this philosophy as naturally as one grows his own mind without even thinking about it. But as young Americans we couldn't stay nourished on the seeds which had given us our beginnings. Like any growing plants we had to extend the purpose of the seeds and evolve our own entity. In trying to protect us from the horrible lessons they learned in their time our parents have truly doomed us to repeat mistakes.

After I had been in Vietnam for a while I (and many others) could not continue to feel that it was my generation's war. The justification that would make it so never arrived once we got there. We began to realize that we came filled more with a sense of obligation than with honest purpose. We became disenchanted with our mindless patriotism rather soon because we had not been completely sold in the first place. From my dove's perch now perhaps I am once more subject to the same foibles and poor eyesight, in reverse, and I am seeing American foreign policy as mostly negative, when it is not necessarily. At least now I think I understand the name of the game and have the human distinction of playing both sides with a vengeance. I think my generation may arrive later at its "own war" (perhaps really a holy war), but this isn't the stimulus in Vietnam.

After I returned from Pleiku to Saigon I vividly remember previewing a videotape of a pro-Vietnam march which had been held in New York. This march was itself a protest to an earlier march which had been held in New York to protest American policy in Vietnam. It was good to see my home town again, from so far away, and I was mostly paying attention to sentimental landmarks on Fifth Avenue that brought lonesome nostalgia to my mood. Though I wasn't really attending to the point of the march, something began to irritate me profoundly. I was vaguely reminded of some Chinese Communist anti-American film that I had recently seen. Suddenly, strutting into my vision across the big television monitor, I saw a middle-aged woman who looked as if she were a grandmother, marching between two small children. Each of her two wards carried plastic submachine guns as they blasted the bowels out of imaginary Vietnamese up and down Fifth Avenue. They looked as intent and happy as any Red Guards carrying "Kill Yankee" placards. The woman carried a sign whose grim message locked my mind until I woke up the next morning, completely lost in myself. In oblivious innocence, wearing the confident smile of the patriot that she certainly was, she waved a banner that read "MY COUNTRY RIGHT OR WRONG." It was a phrase that I had heard all my life. It still seems strange to me that I had never stopped, at length, to think what it implied.

I was left with a terrible taste in my mind, and suddenly found myself diametrically opposed to the pro-war propaganda which I had been busily composing and propagating for the Department of Defense. My disorientation could not have been more sudden had I woken up to find myself Kafka's metamorphosed cockroach, still inhabited by my own mind. I began to feel and ponder my thoughts gingerly, as if they were insect's tentacles at my new, ugly command. Abandoning *all* the resolve that had kept me going was terribly uncomfortable. I don't think I will ever forget the panic at being isolated, not by someone else's views, but by my own. The most frightening thing about this new unwanted attitude was that it was the logical conclusion to everything that I had thought before. Everything that had been said about her enemies seemed now to apply to America too. The more I thought about it, the less I could distinguish "Hanoi Hannah" from my news shows in Saigon on Armed Forces Radio and Television. Just who the hell was doing the right thing? More than that, who was doing anything different from anyone else? Where was my heritage now to come and save me from this huge doubt? It was my *own* propaganda that had made me see it. As I groped for examples to refute myself they only served to back up this exploding picture of sad equality between my country and those that disagreed with her. The wave of disgust in myself was only given strength when I tried to put it all out of my mind or think back for more justifications for why I shouldn't think the way I suddenly did. But now it was exactly those same thoughts which made this all possible. My head was trying to defeat its own best efforts with more of the same thing. The truths of my own inescapable conclusions came bubbling to the top as if from a stranger's head. They seemed foreign, yet they were all too close. There was no contradiction here!

I couldn't help but internally stare at the political dupe I had made of myself. My government hadn't really done it. My officers hadn't done it. My family hadn't done it. I had done it with the skill that only I could use on myself. This was no peace marcher or presumed outright coward that I heard talking in my head. It didn't have the voice of some outside mental adversary whose arguments were easily brushed off by my articulate confidence that we were probably doing the right thing realistically. This was me, and it was no longer gnawing. It was fast becoming my whole basic attitude with the same strength that all my prior convictions had bound me with. So this was the result of my self-consuming head game. The logic which had given the other position force had completed the circle with a finality that was certain. The dominoes of all my prior beliefs about this national direction came rattling down in a heap as the first block to my entire war thought-pattern was innocently knocked over by the last of the same pattern.

It later came to me that the pacifists who had disagreed with me earlier about the war were the innocent victims of their sincere beliefs. It had been so easy for me to call *their* brand of patriotism unpatriotic, but now I saw they were truly the result of—and not a revolution against—their background. This new dovish patriotism was the rightful heir to the patriotism of World War II. It was the same love of country and man which had led them logically to what they felt today. There was no contradiction, no break in the chain. When I heard an old sergeant tell stories about the war in the Pacific it was obvious that he was not a murderer. The entire pulse of his generation concluded that this, and only this, was the right thing to do by all it knew to be right in accordance with the patriotism that preceded it. Today's youth has the lessons its fathers' generation gave them to draw upon to conclude something new and yet something the same.

A more studious sociologist could go back and cite my generation's incubation in the immense communication network of mass media as at least part of the origin of my generation's attitude about its world. Though a young man's whole culture is the same as his father's, at the same time it is altogether different because his father's generation had, in turn, changed the environment it found itself in when it was young. Each generation brings about certain creations: different morals, refined religions, evolved politics, subtler patriotism, and generally newer ways of looking at things. Suddenly it is discovered the boy is different, his views are different. How amazing. All at once there is a big mystery as to how it happened, when there is no mystery at all. The patriotism of the pacifist looks like the complete opposite of that which came before it when it is really the same thing. Spring looks completely different from its father, yet it is the natural result of the winter that gave it birth, and who is to say when spring really stops and summer then begins? And a generational gap is said to exist.

Were it not for this mythical generational gap, mankind would still be in caves. It is not a curse, but rather the very reason for our existence as a species. In a way it is our immortality. Politically my generation has chosen peace, though it is not really even our choice. Our fathers' generation chose peace as well, though they sought it in a different way—the goal was still the same. The eventual contradiction of killing in order to stop killing is extremely hard for today's pragmatic youth to believe in. The sophistication of my generation cannot believe in this paradox as necessary, let alone effective, because our parents gave us a more questioning kind of mental attitude as a legacy with which to challenge the status quo. We can't do anything else, really, so we try to "improve" ourselves as best we can with the equipment we have to do it with.

I came back from Vietnam very changed, and yet still the same. For me it took one instant for all the fragments of my beliefs to come together and bring a change of opinion that paradoxically condemned those same beliefs. But there was a long period after this change of opinion when I felt I was lost, until I realized that was what it felt like when you knew where you were. I've found out many things about Americans as I've discovered many things about myself. In believing this I find that I now look around me with perhaps a little more understanding and compassion than I did before. I can now regard people whom I used to consider enemies as possible friends, for no matter how secure they may seem, I'm now convinced they are as confused as the rest of us. I know at least I'm no better or worse off than they. We are really all in the same thing together.

When I landed back in California at Travis Air Force Base after my year in Vietnam, it was the same 18th day in June it had been the year earlier. The weather, the place, the hour were the same . . . yet everything had changed. About half the soldiers on the plane were the same ones who had been with me going in the other direction that twin day a year earlier. We had all separated to our different units, I hadn't seen any of them for exactly a year, but here they were again. They were obviously the same people, and yet they didn't look the same. The boys' faces were no longer boys' faces. Experience had replaced innocence, and sureness sat where anxiety had once flashed. The other half—well, they just weren't there, and the hushed presence of *their* absence was partly responsible for the new look on the faces of those of us who were left.

TWO

AT HOME

I

During my last few months as a soldier in Vietnam I had been greatly concerned with whether or not I would extend my tour there for an additional six months. The Defense Department had offered a new deal in January 1967, giving servicemen there a free thirty-day leave if they would extend for another six months' duty in Vietnam. For soldiers who were not in too much danger at the time it was an attractive offer. The pay was fantastic and by "free leave" the Defense Department meant that the government would pay for travel and living expenses anywhere in the world. The leave would be exclusive of travel time, so the thirty days started when you arrived at your destination, and worked the same on the way back. The six months naturally did not include the leave, so that started when you returned to war from Tahiti or wherever.

I knew a sergeant who decided to go with that program and picked as his leave destination a little island off the coast of Africa. It took a twelve-day train ride through India and a ten-day boat ride to reach the island, and there his thirty days started. With his choice of geography, he managed to get fifty-four days off out of the junket. I just wanted to go back to the U.S. for the leave, but I had another problem. My time in the Army was getting so short that by the time I returned from the leave and served the six months in Vietnam, my discharge date would have come and gone two months before the extension of duty was over.

In order to make the pieces fit together I would have to apply for a change in my status in order to keep myself on active reserve during that two-month period. Being in Vietnam meant a great deal to me, enough so that I embarked on the sea of paperwork necessary to make this change. But the red-tape tangle was too much; I finally gave up, decided to relax and let myself be rotated home after my year in Vietnam and serve the remaining four months in stateside duty. As far as Vietnam was concerned, I was certain I would make it back there in a year or so as a civilian and I could arrange that better if I were in the States.

Through friends I had made in Vietnam I managed to have my rotation orders set up to assign me to Washington, D.C. After being in the tropics for a year I was yearning for a breath of the East Coast days of my youth. It would be nice to be able to drive home to New York on weekends and relate to something back in the East again.

I left Vietnam in June 1967, and after thirty days' leave, I reported for duty in Washington by mid-July. My career in Army Information had run the gamut from giving tours of the Presidio in San Francisco (through the eighteenth-century fort at the base of the Golden Gate Bridge) to radio and television for the Armed Forces in Vietnam. Sometimes I had been in serious danger, flying over forward positions in helicopters—once I was within seconds of being killed—but a great deal of the time I was perfectly safe. Sometimes I spent days and weeks on boring and tedious assignments, but often enough the work was very stimulating. Now, here I was, a specialist fourth class in the United States Army, Chief Office of Information. My section was Command Information, which had apparently been evicted out of the Pentagon. The space that the section had occupied in the Puzzle Palace had been replaced by a Coordination branch which became the middle man after my section had been banished to a run-down building in the Washington Navy Yard. The continual output of government phones kept us all in constant contact.

As long as I was in Vietnam, in spite of my conversion from hawk to dove, I did not indulge myself in any overt exercise of this attitude. I was spending a great deal of my time with Army news broadcasts, and it was up to me to compile and edit the news items which came in on the UPI and AP wire services. I was not interested in playing up the items where U.S. youths were burning their draft cards, not to mention the flag, for the ears of wounded veterans in the local hospitals. I did not feel so militantly dovish that I would stress the antiwar movement in news programs directed to any of the U.S. soldiers, wounded or not. I had been long enough in the Army to feel bound in its brotherhood and I had no desire to make the men miserable who were already in Vietnam. Some of the antiwar stuff was included; we did not exactly censor the news. But the emphasis could be placed as our own judgment indicated. When I was in Washington I felt this Army brotherhood much, much less. And when I began to meet civilians of my own age I became increasingly drawn into their brotherhood. This matter of fraternity, even when it is quite informal, can be a powerful force.

My first friend in the office was a young fellow who worked alongside of me. Phil was a free-lance writer in his spare time and right then he was doing an article about Ian Fralich, the young leader of a Washington hippie movement. The conversation soon branched out to marijuana, and the exchange of experiences and opinions began. Phil seemed relieved to have someone to talk to in the small unit, so we started continuing the conversations after work. With my tales of marijuana in Vietnam he thought me very hip. He suggested that I should meet Ian, and because I had such an affinity with the whole hippie movement he asked if I would help him with the article. In this connection I soon met Ian and, as is common in a meeting like that, our first exchanges were about drugs as well as philosophy in general and our backgrounds, if not credentials, to back up the subjects mentioned. I had been in Washington only a few days and I was already plugged into a few people who thought somewhat the way I did. This did a lot to relieve the peculiar isolation that was disturbing me.

At that time I occasionally went to the famous store, the Source, which Ian operated, but I saw very little of him. This store, like several others in D.C. and in cities and towns throughout the country, is called a "head shop" by its customers. The word "head" is an all-purpose term which could denote a person who is a liberal, flexible personality. Many young people would say Senator Eugene McCarthy is a "cool head." It is commonly supposed that marijuana users buy and sell marijuana at head shops, but it would be easier to buy it in the main post office because the police keep these shops under constant scrutiny. The Washington *Post* recently editorialized on the subject, charging that the expense of the surveillance was ridiculously out of proportion to the value of the quarry. Of course, the harassment, in itself, strengthens the bonds of the hippie's affection for his favorite head shop. Just as a sports enthusiast expects to find all his paraphernalia for sale at one location, the hippies feel they should be able to find the artifacts which interest them available in one place. Therefore, the Source was stocked with books, posters, protest buttons, music, paint, beads, pipes, light refractors, guitars, kites, underground newspapers, etc.

The economics of hippiedom is much like the economics of any part of society. At the level of "straight" society where extravagant parties, yacht cruises, and other conspicuous consumption is visible, most of the money spent is related to an inheritance from an earlier generation. Among those who are a part of this scene there are some self-made people, some wage-earners. Around the edges are the hangers-on who subsist on pensions from home and whatever loose crumbs they can pick up. The most envied wage-earners are those who engage in the more glamorous trades: fashion, show business, art, music, communications, etc. Their earnings seem to be acquired by flair rather than diligence.

Likewise in the hippie community, the consumption of expensive drugs in attractive settings is dependent upon some rich person's indulgence. Tim Leary has had wealthy sponsors who contributed money accumulated in an earlier generation. Augustus Owsley Stanley III has become almost a patron saint to the hippies. Owsley, as they call him, inherited money. He is a proficient chemist (once a student at UCLA) and it is estimated he has manufactured over ten million doses of LSD, most of which he distributed free to his hippie friends over several years, throughout the United States. Although Owsley was "busted" he is free at this time because he can afford elaborate legal advice. He has been generous in helping others less fortunate. Some hippies make a modest living working part-time selling marijuana. It is such a basic commodity for them that there is a steady if not very lucrative market. In another time they might have worked part-time selling Fuller brushes, door-to-door—or anything at all which demands similar talents.

Phil was a very earnest young writer, and I was then planning to do a kind of photo-essay book with a photographer friend who had taken some spectacular color slides in Vietnam. We talked about various writing ideas he had and, of course, we had the Army in common. Every once in a while I would drop by Ian's just to talk with him or buy a pipe—to smoke some of the Vietnamese marijuana I had brought home. One night I helped him move into the farmhouse he had rented in Virginia. Phil had told me Ian was being watched by the D.C. narcotics agents, but for some reason it never bothered me to walk into his store while in uniform or park my car next to where he lived.

After I had been in Washington a few weeks I came to my office one morning and Phil asked me if I knew how to get in touch with Ian because the photographer who was going to illustrate Phil's article about Ian for a Washington magazine needed to get some shots of him. When I couldn't raise him at the farm or at his store, the photographer called the police department from the magazine office to see if Ian had been arrested—an ever-present possibility. Someone at the police department, perhaps thinking this was a news reporter, told the photographer Ian had been arrested and there were agents on the way to Ian's store to clean it out. At least this was how the photographer heard it and how it was relayed to me. Later I called the store again to check on whether it had been raided, and that was when I realized that the photographer had been given premature and inaccurate information. Thus when I called the store the police had not yet arrived. I left my name with the person who picked up the phone and when the police did arrive soon after, they were told a fellow named John Steinbeck had phoned and warned them the police were on the way. The following day the police were more effective and they raided the Virginia farmhouse, arresting Ian there. He was charged by federal narcotics officials as well as Virginia police for growing marijuana on the farm. With Ian in jail the District police and the federal drug-abuse officers decided to tidy up the loose ends from the day before.

My little mistake in timing the phone call brought me to my first confrontation with narcotics officials. The police had taken note of the name and they were quick to discover I was in the Army. On the second day after the raid on the store the police got in touch with me via the Army.

As one does about most periods laced with mild panic, I remember quite clearly that hushed day when I was summoned to the Criminal Investigation Department office of the Military Police. There I was to exchange information with my brothers-in-arms in the military and also with the civilian authorities. Through conversations with Ian and talks with other friends of mine who have been watched by narcotics agents because of suspected marijuana use I was pretty well informed about the more blatant methods of maintaining a nationwide marijuana paranoia. But this first interview was instrumental in giving me at least some insight into the sincere motivations which keep the life of a narcotics agent full of a sense of self-righteousness in his battle against what he feels to be the "killer weed." It was also the baptism by fire which helped give me the official credentials later for the dubious role of an accepted expert on marijuana.

That particular morning had only just gotten under way at my Army office, following the usual staff meeting designed to remind us, lest we forget, that we were in the Army. I was busy writing one of two official obituaries for the deaths of President Truman and General Eisenhower. Though neither of them was dead the obituaries were to be ready, as they say in the automobile-warrantee business, whichever one came first, in six months, or thirty thousand miles. I was researching General Eisenhower's more inspiring moments of wisdom and courage, that is to say, those moments which the Office of Information found most palatable and suited to their present needs. I was hunting for those clichés and patriotic historical precedents which would give ghostly support to the Vietnam effort. Once the obituary had been completed, and the appropriate time arrived, it would be handed out and reprinted thousands of times by Army News Features as a scoop of the General's death. The more exact details with the dates, times, and places would be filled in the blank spaces. Thus we would guarantee Army publications would properly mourn our hero with the speed and tactical planning his "great leadership" and military mind would surely appreciate, even after death. Beyond this, the color guard from the Military District of Washington was already practicing his funeral march and we just had to make some sort of competitive gesture. Esprit de corps.

Somewhere in my research—about the time when the General was sending the 101st Airborne Division on the first wave of assault at Normandy, giving the stirring Order of the Day as "Full Victory . . . Nothing Else"—the phone rang. The call was from the Criminal Investigation Department of the Military Police. With no further information I was told to report to an Officer Moody at nearby Fort Myer. I was not to take my car; I was to be driven in an Army staff car. With the General's advance obituary as the keynote, the rest of the day was spent tracing a series of tragic absurdities and misunderstandings which became more and more disturbing to me in their ramifications, long after that morning's bout with the Normandy invasion had passed.

Paranoia, with all its bizarre characteristics, is one of the most powerful tools used by a bureaucratic agency to catch anybody at anything. Yes, I had been found out, of that I was certain, but I couldn't for the life of me think what it actually was that had been discovered. In my mind I knew I couldn't be arrested for having smoked marijuana, or saying I had smoked marijuana, or being with people who did smoke marijuana. Yet my mind still went racing back over the list of real and unreal liabilities, one or several of which had caused this summons. Even other people's crimes became deeply intimidating to my memory and I suddenly felt personally responsible for anything I had even heard about.

My somewhat exceptional habits in Vietnam came flooding back as I tortured myself with the extravagant possibilities of the Vietnamese government ordering my extradition to Asia. Visions of a firing squad in some Saigon square filled my mind for a brief moment. When I could conjure up nothing worse I finally began to be rational, and I cast around for ways to be mentally armed for the Criminal Investigation Department's questions. But I couldn't guess what the questions might be and thus preparations were impossible. The phone call had come and I couldn't change its reasons now. It would be better if I relied on spontaneous honesty and abandoned this soliloquy of general guilt I was otherwise subconsciously practicing. I decided to participate rather than perform. If I went in genuinely guileless, perhaps they wouldn't find out all the nefarious deeds my mind was clawing up excuses for.

The staff-car driver couldn't find the Criminal Investigation Department's office at Fort Myer, so taking my suddenly precious liberty in hand, I told him I could walk and get there sooner. Once he had driven off I felt the urge to bolt and run away to Mexico or something. My God, what conscience will do to reason!

Though his name had conjured up images of rare sternness to my now terribly paranoid mind, Warrant Officer Moody was a very warm and friendly man. When he heard I had arrived he came briskly out of his office and greeted me. He shook my hand firmly and asked me to have a seat in the outside waiting room. He told me two other men were coming shortly. With the comment "It's nothing serious," he gestured to an armchair and graciously handed me a *Life* magazine with a cover story on LSD-25. I think I groaned. He left the room.

I was grateful my duty uniform was civilian clothes. With my dark suit and attaché case, I felt much more at ease speaking to any authority. Subliminally, it would be harder to be intimidated in this classless uniform than if I had been in the costume of a mere specialist fourth class in the United States Army. After I had been given sufficient time to sweat (about twenty minutes) two men came through the front door. They stopped at the desk where a soldier met them and buzzed Officer Moody. Once again he came rushing out of his office, signaled me, and the four of us filed into a small room with a sign on the door which read: "QUIET—INTERROGATION IN PROGRESS."

The room itself was only sinister to anyone whose imagination might have made it sinister. It turned out we were all dressed in dark suits; we might have been there to talk over an insurance policy. This atmosphere didn't last long, however. At first, because of my suit, the civilians weren't sure I was Steinbeck. There was an awkward moment or two when they just stood there and waited, presumably for Officer Moody and me to send for the "accused." Moody's casual manner toward me did nothing to clarify this point. The two civilians were perhaps more used to browbeating long-haired teen-agers. I flatter myself in recalling the zeal which went out of their eyes when I broke the silence and introduced myself. With this piece of information they both turned to me and made a gesture as if they were going to cross themselves. Then, in unison, they repeated a litany which told me they were both narcotics agents and two badges flashed briefly as they fairly saluted me with them. Almost as if lighting an ancient torch, the Olympian games of federal interrogation commenced.

The shorter of the two investigators introduced himself as Agent Parnetta of the Federal Bureau of Drug Abuse. He gruffly removed his jacket and straddled one of the straightback chairs with an air of such sordid intent I could only think of José Ferrer just before he pinches Peter O'Toole's nipple in *Lawrence of Arabia*. The taller of the two agents reached out to shake my hand and introduced himself as Agent MacKinnon of the District of Columbia Narcotics Squad. He went over to another chair at a center table and sat down with quiet ease. He kept his neat jacket on and gave me a tremendously understanding look, as if he were sorry and wished his partner would display more *élan* and breeding. Agent MacKinnon seemed to be almost pained by the ordeal as the fingers of his hands came together calmly and were laid politely in his lap. With his light, thinning hair and glow of kindly wisdom, he looked a little like a cosmopolitan Roy Rogers. After having belched once or twice, the short Mr. Dynamic on my right said, "You know where we're from. We have some information about you. But I guess you know why we're here." I tried to register nothing at all. "Are you a friend of Ian Fralich?" was his first question.

I thought to myself that with the exception of the phone call to Ian's store, for the photographer, I hadn't been in touch with Ian since the night at the farm several weeks earlier when I'd helped him move in. I had since read in the newspapers about his arrest at the farm, of course. In describing the arrest the Washington *Post* reported the farm was growing over a hundred thousand dollars' worth of marijuana which was about to be harvested, until the police raided the premises and went gamboling through the grass themselves.

I once saw several acres of the plant burned in southern California by Internal Revenue officers. The area had been roped off and it was fascinating to watch people flock to the site—some with tears in their eyes not caused entirely by the smoke. Jokes flew as what seemed like the whole neighborhood got "high" around the inferno. There were a lot of unkind remarks about the uninitiated officers who were wearing Army gas masks while they went about their destruction.

On the rainy night I was at Ian's farm I didn't see any marijuana growing. It later turned out the few immature plants growing there had been killed by an early frost. The leaves from these plants would not have brought in enough money to buy a copy of the newspaper which reported the story. It also turned out they hadn't been planted on purpose, but rather were just volunteering from some seeds which had been discarded in the process of cleaning a package of marijuana leaves for smoking purposes.

At the time of this interrogation I had been in Washington for about eight weeks and I had known Ian only casually, and in fact I did not really count him as one of my friends. Also, because I knew very few of his friends, I asked my investigators how it was my name had come up. Out came my crime. They told me they had received the word from an employee at Ian's store that I, John Steinbeck, Specialist Fourth Class, United States Army, had tried to warn Fralich about the raid on his store the day before he was arrested in Virginia. (It wasn't really until months later I actually put together what had happened and was told the photographer had called the police department and been given that premature flash on the raid.) According to these men now, I had called the store and left word there that Ian was on the verge of being arrested. They also said I had related how many counts and charges the police had against him. As the enthusiasm of this accusation resounded through the small room, Agent Parnetta, who delivered it, started jumping around all the time, emphasizing I wasn't to think for a second I'd be able to pull the wool over his eyes. Before I could say anything at all in reply, he said, "Aw right, let's start again."

To counter Agent Parnetta's obvious disgust with me, soft-spoken Agent MacKinnon kept saying in a spirit of the deepest regret, "Now John, you aren't being charged with anything, you understand . . . " and "You haven't been instructed, John, as to your rights . . . " and "We would do this differently, John, if we were going to arrest you, or anything . . . " and "This is just a nice, informal meeting . . . all we want is some information and we think maybe you can help us." These comments came out with the golden, honey flow of sublime compassion. But almost as if the dialogue had been orchestrated, mild-mannered MacKinnon's pianissimo faded off just when Parnetta's practiced crescendo came thundering back with the new theme of "How many times have you ever copped marijuana at Fralich's store?" I registered puzzlement at that and he came back with "You know what I mean, at that store he calls the Source!" To me, Agent Parnetta's use of the idiom "copped," meaning to buy marijuana, had a funny ring. But the mood at the time was far from funny; he continued by letting me know that he knew "damned good and well" the Source was a main distributing point for marijuana. Agents had been watching it for over a year. As a taxpayer, I found myself a bit resentful about this kind of costly watching, but I didn't complain on those grounds. I said yes, Fralich had told me he was being watched, and that his phone was being tapped, and that he used to see men across the street taking pictures of the store and the people who came in and out. Agent Parnetta looked very hurt at this. He told me in very stressed words I was not very smart, nor up-to-date, and I was crazy if I thought he was stupid enough to risk a good job by doing things like phone-tapping after the recent Supreme Court decision about such conduct. I allowed as how I had read of that decision, but then I'd also read the Hague and Geneva

Conventions without seeing any trace of their impact in the Republic of Vietnam.

The freewheeling tensions of these informal police interrogations—whether self-imposed or otherwise—begin to take on every aspect of a verbal ballet with the person being questioned as the only improvising member of the company. The other two lead players know the choreography very well, and their seemingly different personality parts seldom vary. On one previous occasion I was privileged to be questioned by another federal team; then they were postal inspectors. Perhaps I attract disaster, or court it at least. This is a very real possibility which my family believes to be a definite personality characteristic of mine. I have thought about this subject a great deal and recent events have made me increasingly thoughtful on the subject. At any rate, a girl friend of mine in California owned a record store which also housed a post-office substation. When counting time came around one month, the till from the substation was fifteen thousand dollars short. Determined to find the thief, two postal inspectors questioned everyone who frequented the store. Since I was romantically involved with the acting postmistress, according to any academy training manual my guilt in this affair was obvious. The agents always look their parts. This pair had the same Cinderella-Goliath act I was seeing again with the narcotics agents. It is an act which is very well done. The interrogation is opened with a serious, but false, accusation which gives the person being questioned a certain confidence through the simple feeling of relief that whatever involvement he might have in the incident is nowhere near what he has just been accused of. He then tends to state his true position about the event, just to prove he didn't do anything even resembling the charge. An extreme example of the success of this approach is something like, "No, I didn't kill her. I couldn't have . . . I was robbing a gas station at the time . . . I can prove it!" Recoiling with intimidation from the louder and more aggressive of the two officers, he seeks protection with the "nicer" one. This fellow generates even more confidence by showing a very detectable dislike for his own crude partner, the man who is causing all the discomfort by asking impossible questions. By displaying both respect and contempt for the subject's intelligence, it is easy to bring out his vanity, ego, fear, and foundationless confidence into a highly visible arena. These things become as eloquent and telling about the man's thoughts as any written dossier might be. Anything which is said seems covered with guilt under these circumstances. It is really extraordinarily effective. There was a part-time post-office cashier who was finally discovered with the fifteen thousand dollars, but the experience had taught me a lot about the method I was exposed to now.

Though supposedly that's why I had been brought in to begin with, the interrogation never returned to the fact I had allegedly tried to steal the prey from the trap, by a phone call to the Source. The target very quickly changed from my crimes to my character. What kind of person was I to hang around with people like Fralich? At first I couldn't believe the way the next question was phrased. Agent Parnetta said he was hunting for the answer to why and how it could be I would volunteer for service in Vietnam, and then turn around and associate with the "very scum of the earth" who were subverting all that "Americanism" stood for. It was difficult to reply to this query. Certainly an answer like "I enjoy them" would have sounded a bit shallow under these conditions. The fact that I had been involved with Phil in doing the article on Ian, and had written an article myself about marijuana use in Vietnam—all of this sounded equally weak in the austere little room. Why would I want to write an article on a subject like that? I explained I had met the *Washingtonian* magazine editor at a social gathering where conversation touched on many subjects, including a comparison of social recreation in Saigon *vis-à-vis* Washington. Use of marijuana, along with use of other things, came up very naturally as a topic of conversation because Vietnam can fairly be said to be a marijuana-based culture in the sense that the United States is an alcohol-based culture. The editor asked me to write an article on the subject; I had no plans to write about it until this invitation. The editor and I also discussed topics for other articles dealing with aspects of Vietnam which are not given much coverage in American news media.

Agent Parnetta listened to me with a distracted air, as if I were trying to keep him off the scent. He returned to press me about my friendship with Ian. "You were friends with Fralich, weren't you? It was because you bought marijuana from him, wasn't it? Or, maybe it was because you are like the rest of those dirty stinking hippies. Maybe, deep down, you are just as immoral and disgusting as they are?" As these rhetorical mouthings settled, the quiet, aging MacKinnon came back in cello tones, suggesting that if I knew anything, anything at all, it would go much, much better for me if I spoke now.

All this time the moodless Officer Moody remained staring down at his fingernails, or looking up at the ceiling. Occasionally during the session I almost thought he was going to intervene on my behalf, whatever that might be. He seemed to show a noticeable resentment for these civilians. I thought at times during the proceedings that I could perceive a feeling of genuine military kinship toward me just in his role of being silent. He broke his silence now and then to offer that as far as he knew my record was good, saying this not once, but whenever he felt it was pertinent. Nonetheless the character assassination continued.

Because of the marijuana-in-Vietnam article, it seemed likely I could prove I'd done a great deal of honest research on the subject of young people and marijuana. Of the very limited assortment of defensive comments I had available, my personal concern about the reasons behind the marijuana situation and the people involved was the most comfortable angle I could take in front of these two men. Their only authority stemmed from the fact they were in a position to be spurred on by their own concern to thwart the use of marijuana by American youth. Although I wasn't particularly trying to thwart it, I was interested, as they were not, in the reasons for its use. My attitude of concerned researcher and onlooker was the only suitable posture for me, and I had the notion I might even stimulate them to think a little from a sociological rather than a criminal point of view. By this time the two agents had started to take notes on their little pads. I decided it would be wise if I did likewise.

After I reached down and took a note-pad out of my attaché case, the tone and content of the questions they asked me did take a tremendous shift. With patronizing interest they began to ask me more about how I felt concerning the research I had accomplished so far.

It was indeed my generation that had been indicted here. I told the agents I was interested in hippies or any other contemporaries in the same way, and for the same reasons, I had wanted to go to Vietnam to see them function there. The draftees don't usually take their prize beads or best sandals to the induction centers, but I know from my own experience the group of young men who were inducted along with me included many long-haired hippie types. The word "hippie" has been worn thin with overusage, but it still describes for me a young person who is hip, who is interested and responsive to the latest things going on in the world of youth. I pointed out I had prepared this article about the use of marijuana in the war zone (a zone which Agent Parnetta seemed to regard as hallowed ground) and I asked them if they would conclude those soldiers who used marijuana were "dirty, stinking scum of the earth." They didn't answer. As I began to warm to my subject the strength of my convictions about many aspects of the generation problem restored my poise.

I tried to explain how I thought the young people they called scum and cancers were becoming more and more alienated from any society other than their own mainly because of a lack of faith in the integrity of formal society. I told them I thought most narcotics agents feel morally justified in planting marijuana in the home of a suspected user or seller of the drug, in order to make an arrest stick. When an agent has a lot of undercover information and everyday logic to work with, this kind of tactic no doubt seems justifiable in bringing a "known criminal" to justice. However, this isn't the best way to instill a sense of respect for police virtue in the young people who are all too aware this goes on. If it was for the eventual protection of America's youth from the abuse of drugs this sort of thing was done, the gesture would perpetually work against itself by merely demonstrating the police were no better or worse than the individuals they were crusading against. I said I thought I was a lot closer to these young people, in a far more constructive way, than any narcotics agent could hope to be. Although I had no plans to set up a crusade of my own I believed some understanding of the people involved had first to be gained. I wished the narcotics agents would alter their tactics in order that I, and perhaps other Americans, could be hopeful about the situation. I knew quite a bit about both sides of the situation and I would be glad to try and communicate with both. If I could really understand the actions of young people perhaps I could help to establish some form of liaison with them and the so-called middle-class society that included their parents and the narcotics agents.

I had at one time or another taken all the drugs young people are interested in, and probably more than most. I shared a common feeling with others of my age, had common references, and in some cases common goals. Anyone who thinks young people today who use marijuana are just going through a stage and will grow out of it is very wrong. The beliefs and attitudes which make young people today behave the way they do have the same depth and conviction as those which made their parents go to war a generation earlier. Their energy is the same and can be seen in the rioting in the streets and on the campuses for what many of them *now* think is just and right. And no matter what, their feelings about the world are the result of *their* environment; they did not pick up these ideas abroad; and they were not duped by some Red conspiracy. I told the agents I felt I had no right, as such, to speak for anyone except myself. But I *know* I am not unique. My ideas and actions in the last five years have been a gradual evolution of my own curiosity and imagination; I was never led astray. I have grown up, as I am, a product of American society, and I regard myself as such, and I do not feel I want to revolt against it. But I do not plead for total, indulgent, understanding of myself, or other young people. For example, I would hope that a murderous young person would be apprehended first and understanding brought to bear later.

One does not have to be either a narcotics agent or a marijuana user to know marijuana is being used by a lot of people, and it is very likely here to stay because the people who use it are not dangerous types in the sense an armed robber or a pathological murderer or a corrupt politician might be. Young people—thanks as much to the civil-rights struggle as to any other single factor—are ready to view the established minions of law and order as mere hired hands at best and more often vicious sadists at worst. Programs are proliferating to give police a new image, that of a community personal-relations man. Meanwhile, in most big cities, where most of the kids are, the old image persists, in the North and the South. Thus, the young are quick to see the law can be an ass, and this can be murderously criminal in its effects and results. Young people still tend to adore the idea of fairness, but they will not accept the idea that any given law must be obeyed just because it is the law, whether the subject of the law is marijuana use or whatever. In this respect young people are remarkably like adults, who also tend to disregard laws which are patently stupid or irrelevant. Meanwhile it is common to read where a doctor or a judge speaks out on the subject of marijuana and says the laws are punitive and unfair in proportion to the offense. Marijuana users smile at this, believing firmly there is really *no* offense involved.

Like the policemen, young people, myself included, want to secure a better world to live in. In looking at the world around them, young people use the superior sophistication which their parents and their schools have given them; it is their upbringing which equips them to make the judgments they do, not some strange new rebellious power from elsewhere. Young people often wonder aloud to each other about why the older generation is so uptight about the typically youthful activities of today, but the estrangement continues. Despite this, I said I thought much of the alienation could be stopped if young people could see what they wanted in many cases were the same things the older generation wanted; things just look different on the outside. As far as the extreme dropouts were concerned, I was, in fact, desirous of exactly what any parent professed to want. I, too, wanted many of the more apathetic ones to come back and function constructively in their own way, just as I would like to see some of my alcoholic adult acquaintances come back from their pathetic escape.

The agents made so many allusions to what they termed the "bad" element of American youth that I pressed them for more definition. It seemed they seriously considered many of the current fashions of young people to be absolutely wicked; they were ready to associate evil with many things any sane person must realize are nothing more than fads and styles of the times. I found myself wondering if Agent Parnetta had worn pegged trousers and a duck-tailed haircut some years earlier; and if he had, had he been cruelly criticized for this or not? At any rate he now made it clear that long hair, beards, beads (or worse yet, bells), guitars, folksinging, sandals or bare feet, were all positively identifying marks of the beast. Any combination of even two of these appurtenances would be interpreted as an absence of morals and presence of the internal decay a good narcotics agent must attack. Agent MacKinnon took a much milder view: he felt many of the things young people did would be all right except for the one thing—drugs. I found myself wondering what was in his medicine chest. If he is anything like the average person today I think it is likely he does not docilely accept whatever state of mind or of blood pressure he finds himself in on any given

day. If he is average I would think he has used either tranquilizers or pep pills of some kind; this seems especially likely for
a narcotics agent because I'm sure they are subject to considerable nervous tension. I found myself talking about the banal,
if true, fact that the last twenty-five years have seen enormous
strides being taken in the use of prescribed medication for
every human affliction. I recalled the thalidomide scare and
the older people inquiring how could it be that this drug, this
tranquilizer, would have been prescribed for pregnant
mothers? Some older people were no doubt well acquainted
with sleeping pills, but apparently they had no idea, in spite
of all the publicity about Miltown *et al.*, that physicians
regularly prescribe medication nowadays to alter and improve the consciousness of their patients. It is no longer considered necessary to passively accept one's state of mind or
body, and since Medicare I'm sure the oldest of the older
generations are fast becoming hip to all the new drugs. The
young people who are exploring hallucinogens are not really
divorced from any other people. And news stories make it
plain a great number of not-so-young people are likewise exploring the field. Perhaps the thalidomide scare (and other
drug and insecticide scares) encourages many of us to think
prescribed medications are not necessarily safe, and all others
unsafe. Insofar as marijuana is concerned the user's own experience is convincing proof it is not dangerous at all.

Agent MacKinnon tried to bring me back to his point,
which concerned the illegality of drugs and the fact that kids
were using illegal drugs, etc. I said I thought people do pretty
much what they have to do to get what they want. Young
people who want to use drugs do not have the secure param-
eters of adults within which to operate; adults who want to
use a drug can fairly easily procure it straightforwardly from
their own physician. If this is not possible, a friend or a friend
of a friend comes through with some pills obtained on some
other person's prescription. Likewise, the hippies have developed their friends in need. I think one of the most striking
characteristics among young marijuana users and sellers is

that the stuff is often given away by one to another and when it is sold the profit margin is very slim. This aspect has kept the Mafia stymied, for they can see no chance of competing, let alone cornering the market. Commonly, some student will take a vacation trip to Mexico and bring back a suitcase full of the stuff for himself and his friends. The cost of the trip and the booty will be evenly divided among all. Perhaps that is communistic, in a way, but not the way Agent Parnetta thinks. I know Ian had a dream of this farm in Virginia being a place where he could eventually raise a lot of marijuana which he would sell in his store, but I know he would have prided himself on keeping the cost at a minimum. Adults may not really believe this attitude, but they will fail to understand what is involved if they refuse to believe it.

I asked Agent Parnetta how it could be that if marijuana was such a vicious substance the Asians had been using it with no demonstrably ill effects for centuries. I have never heard of anyone trying to equate marijuana use in India, for example, with anything at all. Our whole concern has been to feed Indians. If anyone thought they could be improved by not being allowed marijuana (and all the more concentrated marijuana products, such as hashish) it seems likely there would have been some report on the subject. Agent Parnetta perked up at this and said he was sure a lot of the problems in Asia might very well be improved if marijuana was stamped out in the Orient. I could just picture him straining at the leash, eager for an assignment out there where he could really go to work, wholesale, with no need to scout around for weeks and months before he pounced on a suspect.

In Vietnam today people suffer from a kind of black-and-white thinking; every person has some definite enemy. These agents reminded me of that because to them the hippie subculture was a threatening enemy force, and this belief could fill some of them, apparently, with a positively religious zeal. I think of myself as a religious person and, in a way, I had to respect their fervor. As the conversation became increasingly far-reaching, the agents made veiled comments about just who was behind "all this." Apparently they fancied a complex global Communist strategy with its American origin in "Red-infested" Berkeley. From that campus the Communists and their sympathizers had carried this plague subtly and deliberately. The Communists had sent out Pied Pipers who seemed appealing, garbed in casual clothes, wearing longish hair, decked out with beads, only to seduce and ensnare innocent young Americans into adopting the same kind of outfits. I tried to argue with Agent Parnetta on that score and I assured him the kids developed their personal styles themselves—much as they have developed their own musical styles. Serious sociological studies have underscored this fact, but I'm sure Agent Parnetta would suspect any sociological study that even dealt with young people's clothes and music. After the Piper had the kids in his spell there was the big clincher—when the charmed youngsters were "started on dope." I tried to argue that point a bit, too, assuring Parnetta that nobody "started" me using marijuana any more than I was "started" on tobacco, in the sense that I was coerced in any way. Force doesn't say much to kids. I suggested he should know better than anyone that law-enforcement officers have not gotten very far trying to force young people to give up marijuana. (Oh yes, the global tactics were supposed to reach out to young Americans through the brothels of Korea and Vietnam.) I wished I had my article already published and could whip out a copy of the magazine and say, "Read this! You don't know how it is in Vietnam!" But I realized these dedicated civil servants had become witch-hunters and they thought they were fighting for their very existence now, not to mention their salvation later. They were quite beyond being able to receive much information, let alone new ideas. Perhaps the ideas of many young people today (perhaps even of the agents' own children) were indeed burning out the roots of the witch-hunters' own existence. I found myself hoping that very possibly this was the case and in that sense the agents were correct.

Parnetta brought me back to what he considered the point with a resounding declaration that people like Fralich weren't fit to live in American society—"He should be locked up and put away for a long, long time." Knowing Fralich and thinking of other hippie friends, I had a hard time making this agent's expert opinion and attitude fit the image of "friends of youth" that the agents also professed to be in carrying out their duty to protect all the kids in the country. Parnetta continued by saying people like Fralich were really no better than animals. People like him preferred to live in the woods and country like beasts and thus they should be treated that way. It was tempting to counter this with some classic tale of woodland idylls, but I did not. At this point some heavy references were made to my family and upbringing and the question was raised again—how could I be acquainted with such dreadful types? It was sounding like a witch hunt more and more but with me as the kindly old gravekeeper. I could think of no adequate reply to those questions but I was satisfied that both agents were considerably frustrated by the responses I did make. It was much easier for them to grill teen-age flower children, who are usually quite intimidated by any kind of police, than it was for them to undermine my poise. I may have been trembling before this investigation began but as it proceeded I felt definitely nourished and in good health. At some point they realized that, and when they did the whole business came to an end quickly. They told me they would appreciate any information I thought would help them, and Officer Moody suggested that since I was in the Army I could pass anything on to him and he would give it to the proper authorities. The meeting ended and I went back to work.

Had things gone a little differently and had I never been connected with Ian by the police, it is quite likely that my already short association with Ian would have fizzled out completely when I met new friends in Washington. But Agent Parnetta and Agent MacKinnon had tied me to Ian, if with nothing else than their incredible hatred for him and the people who were like him.

After his Virginia arrest, Ian was let out on fifteen thousand dollars' bail within a few days. Somewhere along the line Ian had met a liberal-minded older woman who appreciated the flower-child philosophy. She said she found it and marijuana far less harmful than the juvenile-delinquency era of switchblades, tire irons, and bicycle chains she had been brought up in. She was very wealthy, I was told, and she put up the bail for Ian to be released pending his arraignment in Virginia.

The next time I saw Ian, I ran across him in the street. Perhaps we *had been* tied together by the police, or perhaps it was just because I was beginning to like him, because of his soft, unaggressive approach to life and to the police. For whatever reason we found ourselves embracing each other in the street like old friends who had been through a battle together. He told me how the arrest had taken place out at the farm and I told him the bizarre misunderstanding the police had with themselves by the early-warning episode. I asked him to come visit me sometime and he said he would. I had an apartment in downtown Washington about a block from the White House.

One night in October there was a knock at my door and Ian came in. He told me he didn't have any place to stay because all his friends who would have put him up were afraid that by having him there they would attract too much attention from the local narcotics officials. They much preferred smoking their marijuana in peace to putting up the fellow who had gotten it for them. Being counter-suggestible, I immediately invited Ian to stay with me. His girl friend, Nancy, whom I had met the night he moved to the farm, had left to spend some time in New York with a third member of Ian's tribe, Jeanie. Although my apartment was small he was all alone and there was certainly room for him. Somehow, I also welcomed the chance of getting back at Agents Parnetta and MacKinnon by flaunting Fralich in my home.

Of course, my original intentions were to keep the place clean of marijuana, but that was a philosophical and physical impossibility as it turned out. It was during this period of about a week and a half of living with Ian that I really got to know him, and in so doing got to know a great deal about myself. I had already made the leap from one of the millions of marijuana smokers to one of the thousands of marijuana smokers who were in contact with the police. The idea of going to jail was beginning to be a daily, if passing, thought. My exposition to the agents about the character of the hippie had begun to work its way on me as one of the incontestable flaws in American thinking about Americans. It occurred to me that going to jail for marijuana would, in ten years, be no shame or crime at all and I was almost looking forward to being part of the future-oriented philosophers, like Gandhi. I felt almost it was a little bit of Purgatory I would have to go through in order to stand up for the things I thought were right.

A recent newspaper editorial had played up the notion of Moscow and Hanoi being implicated in a Red conspiracy which was shipping drugs, marijuana especially, to the cream of our American youth. We joked about some hippies we knew who were going to write Ho Chi Minh, Mao Tse-tung, Fidel Castro, and the East Germans, urging them all to ship all kinds of stuff, LSD included. As long as the establishment was going to believe in such a plot, it was a shame not to benefit from the possibility.

But Ian had already been arrested and was waiting for his trial. He was almost certain to get a few years, and here I was, the conceptual dilettante in front of a guy who was really on the verge of going through with it. In trying to cheer him up about it, or at least point out some of the merits of going to jail, the time I spent with him during the next few days were almost entirely filled with discussing the laws about marijuana and the possibility of living in jail.

Ian had told me he would only be staying with me for a few days, two weeks at the most. His girl friend, Nancy, and

Jeanie were soon to be back from New York and they would find some place for all of them to live. Ian needed money, since his farm and store had been liquidated by the narcotics agents, but he didn't really want to deal in marijuana any more. From time to time, he would do favors for friends and connect some friend of his with some other friend who had marijuana. He had just such an opportunity to perform this function with twenty pounds which came into his hands. Nancy and Jeanie got back from New York the day the twenty pounds arrived. It was on a weekend and Ian went out to contact his friends on Sunday night. I had gone to sleep early and when I woke up around one in the morning Ian had returned and quite by surprise I was now rooming with Ian, Nancy, Jeanie, and twenty pounds of marijuana. I had told him I didn't want him to bring it to the apartment since after my first interview with the narcotics agents it was quite obvious to me I was being watched. Unknown to me was the fact there was also a warrant out for Jeanie's arrest for selling LSD to an undercover agent in Washington. I quickly went back to sleep rather than endure the waking anxiety about having this stuff in my apartment.

The next day I went to work after telling Ian to get the marijuana out of the apartment immediately. During the time Ian was staying with me I made it clear to my Army friends and supervisors that he was a temporary house guest. They made it clear that this pleased them not at all, but since I was so open about it they couldn't actually forbid me to allow it. That Monday morning Ian had to appear in court in Arlington, Virginia, to be arraigned and have a trial date set. Nancy went with him and Jeanie and the marijuana slept on in the apartment, as I was to learn later. But Ian and Nancy returned before noon and the watchful agents probably followed them right in the door.

Meanwhile, back at my office . . . I was worrying if I would ever make it out of the Army. From the way things were going it was exceedingly chancy. My Army experience had been colorful but a court-martial was never my idea of a good way to broaden my military knowledge. Vietnam had been one of the most stimulating experiences of my life and I had really grown to love part of the Army. But I could find no part of that in the corporate minds that made up the Washington military in which I now found myself swamped for the rest of my time. This was the Public Relations Army with its paranoid vision of what other people thought of its image. The Pentagon and the Army's Information Office didn't have the magnetic motivation of the Army in the field. There was no gleam in the eyes of these gold-buttoned office-workers. Fluorescents and Xerox machines had turned these good people into nine-to-five government employees caught in the paperwork of justifying their own position. The fact that not even the highest-ranking of them really knew what that position was only continued to fuel my bitter opinion of these gleaming big-business executives and their Puzzle Palace headquarters. Smothered by the weight of their own directives and suspicions about each other's intentions, the military in Washington seemed to me connected in no way with the exhausted but clear-thinking independent team that I had left in Asia. What military bearing I might have had was being drained out of me with the superfluous vacuum of self-conscious propaganda I found myself pounding out daily. It had been months since it had occurred to me to salute anyone. Considering my civilian interests, and my growing dissatisfaction with this military madness, prayer seemed the only way to keep out of the federal prison where I just might be headed.

This day seemed the worst, though, when I thought of all that marijuana sitting in my apartment after I had left in the morning. To have made it through Vietnam only to be finished back home was too much for me to bear serenely. I knew something was really wrong when I got home late that day and found my apartment was locked. I felt a little sick when my imagination played with the possibilities. I had called home several times in the afternoon but no one answered. This was bad. My door was never locked. I went back down the stairs to try the fire escape so I could crawl through the kitchen window. There it all was, just as I had known it would be. My "friends of youth," the narcotics agents, had finally come, and my apartment had been busted. From that day on, this shrine of search and seizure would be referred to by the Washington *Post,* and my more sarcastic friends, as the "dope pad."

I was once invited on a marijuana raid in California. When the call came in from the police department, I was the only newsman on duty in the small Palm Springs radio station. The whole idea was embarrassing to me. I had not been very involved with marijuana in this little resort town, but I certainly knew what it was. I just hoped I wouldn't be interviewing any friends on my tape recorder as I went out on the assignment. The reporters and newsmen were briefed at the stationhouse after midnight and then we split up into several patrol cars. The desert "clean-up" was under way. Four homes were raided that night and torn apart. The morning news carried the scandal with headlines that would have been worthy of an ancient exposé of Sodom and Gomorrah. The police told me a pusher they had arrested had made a deal, supplying the police with names of customers in return for leniency for himself. With a blessed stroke of luck all the offenders were strangers to me, but I still felt pretty bad about being a part of all this trouble over such a ridiculous thing. The other newsmen were in good spirits, however, and we joked about how the winter had been pretty dull and the police department needed to show the chamber of commerce that the wheels of law and order, though sometimes silent, were still turning with constant concern for public safety.

From the kitchen window I could see that the week's garbage which had been stacked and sacked neatly was now dumped all over the floor. Everything that had been in the living room was strewn all around and ripped apart. Papers were scattered around and the furniture had been picked up and thrown over in upside-down positions. As I examined the place more closely it was evident some manuscripts were missing, in particular the article on marijuana in Vietnam. There was no question my horror had been someone else's fun. No policemen jumped out of a closet to grab me, so for the moment I was all right, but I felt like I was in the eye of a hurricane.

I couldn't stop thinking about Ian. Poor Fralich; it would be really bad if they had picked him up. Hell, I knew they had him! That's why all this had happened. He was waiting to go to jail anyway. He had just been passing time. It was strange, but only the day before I had said to Ian I thought I would probably spend some time in jail before I got out of the Army. I said I thought it would be interesting and maybe deeply educational. I always liked to travel light, and perhaps I would find out just how little I needed to exist. It looked now as though I might have my mental picture fully realized before I thought the time had come. My research into Washington's marijuana scene had reached a crucial stage overnight. I thought back to that California raid when I had to speak my thoughts into the portable tape recorder. For this raid I silently mouthed the exclamation of my generation: "Wow . . . "

D

I I

In keeping with my usual defense mechanism, my first in-
stincts were to protect myself by going straight to the police
and asking them what had happened. But I was also afraid
that the result of this might be to be arrested on the spot,
which could hardly be called a successful defense maneuver.
Since no agents had grabbed me as I walked into my apartment, and they had taken any evidence that may have existed
anyway, I decided it would be better to have a lawyer who
would get in touch with the police and tell them I was available for any action they wanted to take. I went to the office of
the *Washingtonian* magazine to ask for advice from my
friend Mark Baldwin, the editor there. The magazine had
been doing a story on a Washington lawyer by the name of
Ira Lowe. Mr. Lowe was the American observer at the Castro
trials right after Fidel took over the Cuban government. He
was also the American observer for the Eichmann trial which
took place in Israel. However, his main importance to me
was the fact that Ira Lowe had the only case in the District of
Columbia that had been accepted by the United States Court
of Appeals contesting the fact that marijuana was included
with heroin and other addictive drugs under District of
Columbia statutes although it was not an addictive drug.
Therefore, Lowe's client, in that case, had been arrested with
the enforcement of a medically inaccurate law. This approach
had been tried several times in many states but Lowe's case

was exceptional because his plea had been accepted as worthy of review by the Court of Appeals.

I called Lowe from the *Washingtonian* office and explained my predicament. I told him I was broke and could not give him a retainer and because my name was Steinbeck I wanted to make it clear before he accepted me as a client that I had no financial connection with my father. If he accepted me he would have to wait for his fee until such time as I could pay him. He listened to all this, told me that he would take my case, and I agreed to come over to his office right away.

Unlike most lawyers I had met, Lowe did not immediately assure me that everything was going to be all right and neither did he instantly start running down the million and one legal loopholes most lawyers feel they have at their command. Lowe was an extremely impressive man who was to become one of my close friends. He had obviously earned and deserved his international stature in the somewhat inverted legal world of Washington and other capitals. He didn't talk rapidly, nor did he have the annoying zeal of the typical legal eagle. Lowe has a full beard and fairly long hair which combine to make him look like a youthful patriarch. I got the impression he was more interested in me personally than in the business we would have together professionally. He told me it would be best if I didn't go home that night, and stayed with Mark Baldwin instead, in order to avoid being arrested before he could contact the police for me. He would be in touch with the police very soon and he would explain to them that he was representing me and advise them I was available at any time either for questioning or arrest. I took his advice and spent the night at Mark's house.

When I arrived at work the next day the papers were full of Ian's arrest at my apartment. However, they had not yet identified the apartment as mine, merely referring to the incident as being seizure of the largest cache of marijuana ever recorded in the District of Columbia at a "dope pad" located at 1737 F Street, N.W. Once again, my "beat 'em to the punch" strategy came into play, and before I'd even gotten my morning coffee I was in my Colonel's office telling him what had happened. I explained that although I hadn't been arrested, or even charged with anything, it seemed inevitable I would be arrested so I had already engaged legal counsel, from a civilian lawyer, rather than from the Judge Advocate General's office. The Colonel was extremely quiet throughout my nervous explanation of how it was the police had arrested a famous Washington hippie with twenty pounds of marijuana in my apartment. After I was through he looked at me for a long time without saying anything. Then very quietly he almost destroyed my entire military bearing by saying, "Well, John—boys will be boys." I couldn't believe it. Immediately reverting to his military vocabulary he thanked me for briefing him on my legal entanglements. He expressed his appreciation for my giving him the information so that he could inform his superiors in advance of being questioned by them himself. Once he was informed, and had all the answers, everything would be all right from his point of view. It wasn't good that a member of his command was on the verge of being arrested, but at least he would have a little time before it happened to make out his report as to why it had happened.

Lowe had advised me to keep away from my apartment, but I thought I'd stop and pick up my mail on the way to the *Washingtonian* office after work that day. I double-parked my car, ran in quickly, and picked it up. I was back in my car, about to put it in gear, when my old friend Agent MacKinnon walked up to the window and knocked on it. As I rolled down the window he asked me if my name was John Steinbeck and I couldn't help but laugh. Without any further ado and before he had a chance to tell me that he had a warrant for my arrest I asked him where I could park my car. Everything was very friendly and he suggested I might like to put it in the parking lot across the street, which I did. In his usual nice way he said that he preferred not to search me on the street and politely said, "You're not carrying anything, are you?" I told him no and that seemed sufficient. I got in his car with two other agents and was taken to the District of Columbia police station and booked on two counts: maintaining a common nuisance (allowing marijuana users to be in my apartment) and possession of marijuana (being the lessee of an apartment where marijuana was found). I asked MacKinnon why I had been arrested on the street when my lawyer had assured the police I was available on request. Apparently when Lowe called the police they did not have a warrant for my arrest and the police had informed Lowe of that fact. After all, these things take time. Some hours later a warrant was made, so there was nothing MacKinnon could do but carry out the warrant. I asked him what would have happened if I hadn't come by for my mail. "Well," he said, in his leisurely manner, "we would have had a very long wait, perhaps." Such are the workings of our legal process.

From the police station I phoned Lowe and reported on my situation. He was annoyed because he had been assured there was no warrant for my arrest, but he was far more accustomed than I to the mechanics of police action. I do not know for a fact that newsmen were informed in advance but they were certainly on hand at the police station and seemed aware I was going to appear. Photographers busily took pictures and the police looked heroic and I looked sinister. On the way to the station MacKinnon told me he much preferred arresting hippies for marijuana than arresting heroin users. No doubt it was much easier for him to intimidate teenagers than tough heroin addicts who had been through the process often enough to have very little awe of the agents. Also, I think a man like MacKinnon would be filled with a sense of saving young souls from a fate worse than death by arresting them on a marijuana charge, whereas the hardened addict would seem to him beyond rescue. The Washington *Post* noted the results of this preferential policy when they observed that the heroin traffic in the District of Columbia had increased more than five times what it had been two years earlier. The policy could be seen as enlightened if harassment of the real addicts was being converted into a concern for them as sick people. Even the hippies would approve this kind of attitude, for the hippies are young and healthy enough to run and the addicts are not. It is highly doubtful, however, that there is any enlightenment involved, but I don't think MacKinnon meant to suggest *that* when he commented on how much nicer it was to arrest hippies.

At the police station I was given a number of forms to fill out with questions like what brand of cigarettes did I smoke, was I married, did I drive a car, etc. I was told that I had to fill them out in order to get to court that night where a trial date could be set. Lowe understood all this, of course, and he agreed to meet me later in court that same night. I filled out the forms and then was taken to jail to wait until Lowe arrived. In many ways I had become used to being in the Army and it seemed strange to be treated as a civilian, in a civilian jail. Apparently MacKinnon had first set out to look for me at my Army office but the military does not permit the arrest of one of its people within an Army compound.

However, because I was in the Army, the Military Police were notified of my arrest and two MP's from the Navy Yard were sent over to take custody of me after I pled not guilty. The judge set a trial date and I was released on personal bond to the MP's without bail being required. The MP's took me to the stockade at the Navy Yard and there I stayed until the next day.

During all the proceedings, the jail was swarming with reporters. Because of my father's name they were busily inquiring about his views on marijuana and his views of my arrest. I explained to them that my father was in the hospital for an operation at that particular moment and I hoped the news of my arrest would not upset his health. Quite unwittingly I started a national scare that John Steinbeck, the author, was on his deathbed. The Washington *Post* headline the next morning read: "Author's son arrested in dope pad while father is critically ill in hospital." My father told me later that a friend of his had received a call from the obituary department of a New York newspaper asking if they should prepare an obituary for the near future. Shades of my own experience with premature obituaries.

The MP's traditionally handle you differently than civilian police. They use a mixture of brutality tempered with the strange kinship which pervades military life. The search procedure involved being kneed in the back, but it was good-natured. The sergeant on duty at the MP station wanted to swap war stories about Vietnam as the guard relieved me of my belt, shoes, etc. After midnight the MP's got in touch with my Colonel, who told them to let me go. But it was a long way back to my apartment, and since my Army office was in the same compound as the MP station, it was decided it would be easier for me to stay there the rest of the night so I wouldn't have so far to go to report for duty the next morning.

When I marched to my office the next day, under MP escort, I felt a little like a Japanese general surrendering on a U.S. battleship. There was the same sense of acting out a superfluous ceremony. Nonetheless it was deadly serious and we went through it deadpan. People peeked out of doors and windows from the various Army offices as we passed by. To the younger soldiers I was already achieving the status of a vicarious hero in a melodrama that they were delighted to have actually happening in their office. Soldiers are always ready for any scandal to keep the bull sessions livened up. This kind of event is important for any group of people who work in closed societies like prisons, universities, and hospitals, as well as the Army. I had managed to create quite a stir within the Army and without. My vision of having a lawyer, and being subsequently questioned in a mannerly and discreet fashion, was apparently naïve if not impossible.

I went into my Colonel's office and said the only thing that would fit the situation: "Specialist Steinbeck reporting for duty, sir." He very cordially inquired how my night had been with the MP's, and I remarked that this was the first day I had actually been to work on time since I'd been stationed there. He laughed indulgently and told me I was to call a long-distance operator in New York because one of my father's lawyers was trying to reach me—he gestured toward his phone. Within the first few minutes of listening to the lawyer I learned I had nothing to worry about—I was assured the lawyer I had engaged was terrible, whereas my father's lawyer was prepared to dig up Clarence Darrow—the Joint Chiefs of Staff were to be notified—the war in Vietnam was going to stop for my trial—my landlady would testify I had never lived in the apartment—and so forth and so on. I remembered this guy from when I was a little boy and he's always affected me in a peculiar manner, making me want to hang up the minute I heard his voice. I knew the last thing my father would want would be to have any special favors done for me or any of his family. Perhaps if I were involved with something I considered really serious—an accidental manslaughter charge, for instance—I would have reacted differently and been hollering for all the help and influence I could muster. But, for all that I was capable of being very concerned about my predicament, I never ever could regard a marijuana offense as truly grave. This may be largely because of seeing marijuana so casually regarded in Vietnam, although long before Vietnam I had not been able to believe that using marijuana was a criminal thing, no matter how the laws defined it. I know only too well that the law is the law, but each of us cannot help but respond to his own sense of values.

I told the New York attorney I already had a competent lawyer and I asked him to convey this to my parents. I hoped my parents would be relieved that I was not in jail, and that I was on reasonably good terms with the Army and my particular section of it. I did learn, however, that my father had heard of my arrest by seeing my picture on the morning TV news while he was lying flat on his back (in preparation for a spinal operation) trying to choke down a hospital breakfast.

Up until this time things had been going so fast I hadn't time to do much but react in a positive way to each turn of events. There was certainly no time for regret. But when I got back to work that day, the first wave of excitement had calmed down and I had time to think. It was all over and yet it was all just beginning. Things seemed even to me to be a little bit more crucial than the usual situations I habitually got myself into (if only to get myself out of them). It was a relief to feel I was being charged with a crime which my own morality and intellect told me was of a very uncriminal nature. Although I had never been charged with an actual crime it was perfectly possible in my imagination that I might happen to be someday. I kept telling myself what I'd told the New York lawyer, that it would have been different if I'd been arrested for robbing a store, even, but here I was —one of thousands of young people in America today— going through a marijuana bust with the smooth bureaucratic paperwork of a traffic offense. I would probably have to embark on a minor crusade to prove myself not guilty. In all the effort which was sure to come in this essentially stupid crusade I would have to work up the same kind of interest and enthusiasm the narcotics agents are fired with in their essentially stupid crusade on the other side.

In spoofing the usual Army technique of selecting a single soldier for some especially good performance, my office had collected all the news clippings from the local papers and mounted them on a big display board with the flag of the newspaper and the pictures, complete. Five or six of these items centered around a large caption which read: "Army News Features, Soldier of the Month, for Action Above and Somewhat Beyond the Call of Duty." This was signed by the officers and men of my section. Later I took this gem to decorate my father's hospital room.

The next morning I went to visit my father in New York. My brother, Thom, had flown to Washington from his Kentucky Army post on leave, and together the two of us drove up in my car. Thom and I are as close and as distant as two brothers can be. His character is not like mine; the environment he makes for himself is not like mine. But we would be immediately joined to each other on a jaunt like this because of our early years together when we were natural allies in numerous battles with our parents. Now we were driving to see them, but I alone was the one with a problem, and because Thom couldn't help but be aware of my current notoriety in regard to marijuana, we began to talk about that. Although he had been casually acquainted with it and smoked it a few times, he had lots of questions to ask me because we had been out of touch in recent years.

Thom was interested in how I had come to write about marijuana in Vietnam and I gave him a sort of résumé of the article which the *Washingtonian* had bought, although at this moment it was still in manuscript form. Rather than paraphrase my résumé I am going to include it here. This version is an expansion of the article which later was published in the January issue of the *Washingtonian*.

III

THE IMPORTANCE OF BEING STONED
IN VIETNAM

> There is, monks, that plane where there is neither
> extension, nor motion, nor the plane of infinite ether,
> nor that of neither-perception nor non-perception,
> neither this world, nor another, neither the moon nor
> the sun. Here, monks, I say that there is no coming
> or going or remaining or deceasing or uprising, for
> this is itself without support, without continuance,
> without mental object—this is itself the end of suffer-
> ing.
>
> *Hinayana* selection

A Commentary Drawn from Personal Experience
and Investigation on the Use of Drugs and Patriotism
in Vietnam

For the time being, very few addictive or "dangerous"
drugs are used in Vietnam by American soldiers or by the
Communists. The only real exception to this is the package
of dextro-amphetamine supplied by the United States Army
in the survival kits given to soldiers in the field. It would not
really be fair to call this drug "dangerous" and its good
service should be obvious to anyone who has ever taken a

"dexie" or any of the amphetamine "pep" pills. However, even though I would not call the drug "dangerous" in mild usage, it is interesting to note that it is always termed "dangerous" if a district attorney is trying to prosecute a domestic case for possession of the pills without a prescription. I remember many an exhausted soldier grinning at the instructions on the back of the package: "These pills are not to be taken without the permission of a Commissioned Officer." The distribution of amphetamines in Vietnam takes place mainly among the rank and file by the young enlisted corpsmen who have access to the sources of supply, and they are passed out with the very definite purpose of helping, not hurting. [After this article was published, I received a number of letters from sailors attesting to their use of amphetamines on the aircraft carriers off the Tonkin Gulf. Here, as in the Army, the pills, originally intended for use in Survival Kits, leak out in great quantities through the personnel who handle them. The letters stressed how the pills had often been life-savers, literally, enabling weary men to keep functioning when they had no choice but to keep going.]

Opium in the Orient is a special tradition in itself, and the carrying out of that tradition is too time-consuming and elaborate for the average GI to bother with. It is also very incapacitating to the novice user. This is not the best condition to be in when confronted with an ambush, terror attack, or some like activity.

After opium, what remains are the fields and jungles of Southeast Asia, including Vietnam, which for thousands of years have been the natural home of the ever-popular *Cannabis sativa,* or marijuana. It has a more powerful brother known as hashish. Despite the fact that marijuana and the purer hashish derivatives from the female hemp plant are as old as time itself, the drug was only recently introduced to white society in Europe in the middle of the nineteenth century [see Appendix I].

Unlike opium or heroin, which are body drugs, marijuana is a mind drug, and you can learn to function quite normally with marijuana. In South Vietnam the best of this plant comes from Cambodia and Laos and the vast bulk of the "good stuff" comes across the border via the Ho Chi Minh Trail, the same route made famous by the Viet Cong—a fairly romantic migration. Thailand sends some into Vietnam with the help of pilots, crewmembers, and straphangers flying Air America from Bangkok. For the Vietnamese customers, like most everyone else, the wine always tastes better if it is imported.

The first question that comes up in a discussion about marijuana with someone who has never smoked it is "How does it feel?" and this is where the vast majority of misinterpretations about any drug starts. Many young American soldiers in Vietnam are very disappointed with marijuana. Those who used it in the States are charmed to find it easily available in Vietnam, but those who grew up with the idea that smoking marijuana was some fantastic experience are often angry that it does not live up to the billing it had in their home town. If a person ordinarily smokes cigarettes and he smokes marijuana in the same fashion, he would notice very little effect. In fact, marijuana might seem to him no more than a brand of tobacco much poorer and less satisfying than the brand he usually smokes. I well remember my first cigarette when I tried to smoke as a child; I was sick and dizzy. Even now, if I do not smoke cigarettes for several days the first one will still make me a bit dizzy. Marijuana smoking, for a non-cigarette-smoker, would produce comparable unpleasant effects. Somewhat deeper inhaling than with cigarettes is necessary to feel anything measurable, but I have heard many soldiers say they felt nothing at all. When the same amount is taken by someone who regularly smokes marijuana the effect is noticeable because the smoker knows what to look for, just as the habitual cigarette smoker does.

If it were just for three or four minutes of exposure, this minor tickle to consciousness has a feeling so vague it could easily be mistaken for normal consciousness. But when marijuana is described incorrectly, using words to define sensations, the sum total of all this word coloring builds up in the imagination of the listener as being a totally disabling chemical barrage to the senses and one's equilibrium. When I think of the language of our cigarette commercials on TV now, I shudder to imagine what the advertising may be when the time comes, which it probably will, when marijuana is being merchandised. Rumors persisted among the soldiers in Vietnam that American tobacco companies were secretly buying up great tracts of land in southern Mexico where the "good stuff" grows, in order to be first on the market with the best when the day came and marijuana was made legal. These led to other rumors that American companies were scouting Southeast Asia for suitable arrangements to import marijuana for the American trade. Some more sophisticated type would counter with a forecast about a tricky, synthetic product, which would mimic marijuana; it would be put on the market to "hook" the users (as marijuana never could).

Soldiers spent a lot of their time talking about marijuana. This gets right to the heart of the matter, for in talking about marijuana, the uninitiated are left with their imaginations to run wild. They supply themselves with often exaggerated estimates of just exactly what the plant does do. The Army doctors and chaplains deliver character guidance talks on the subject, using the most alarming terms. In the few assessments there are in medical literature about psychoactive drugs of any kind, the description of the effects on the nervous system of changing mood, apperception, and other aspects of behavior are couched in medico-psychological terminology which reflects the inappropriateness of technical terms. The phrase "altered consciousness" in connection with a drug sounds frightening but the same phrase could equally well be applied to the effects of taking a steam bath. If a group of women shoppers at a sale were to be described in the same kind of technical terms, an impartial and objective assessment of their behavior would class them in such categories as obsessive-compulsive, paranoid-schizophrenic, and disoriented by temporary psychosis as a result of their inability to cope with approach-avoidance conflicts and multiple-goal-set confusions. With these stock items in the professional phraseology of the psychologist and psychoanalyst it is not surprising that the official, scientific marijuana experiments can be truly alarming. I knew an Army doctor who set up just such an experiment, and he collected a lot of firsthand reports from marijuana users that sounded like the soldiers were describing their escape from the Black Hole of Calcutta. I prefer Baudelaire, who wrote his most accurate prose in describing the effects of hashish on his own mind in *Les Paradis Artificiels,* where he points out that the material for any of the mind's experiences must come from that same mind's store of remembered and imagined sense data:

> Men who are eager to experience unusual pleasures should know that in hashish they will find nothing miraculous, absolutely nothing but what is extremely natural. The brain and organism on which hashish operates give only their ordinary individual phenomena, increased it is true as to number and energy but always faithful to their origin. Man cannot escape the fatality of his physical and moral temperament. Hashish will be for man's familiar thoughts and impressions a mirror that exaggerates but always a mirror.

Soldiers who become barroom brawlers when drunk are not really changed personalities; liquor only frees their repressed urges. Such types may feign ignorance of their actions the following day or indicate great remorse. But basic psychology makes us know that in the long run repressions will out; better to brawl occasionally than to suppress oneself into ulcers, or store it all up until one day you let go and shoot everyone in sight. Likewise, morose drinkers reveal another side of their personalities. Marijuana is comparable in that inhibitions may be released by it; but it has a predominantly soothing effect. Repressions seem to be resolved much less dramatically than with liquor, and there is no hangover. People whose stomachs are easily upset by several drinks usually find that marijuana affects them similarly. Likewise, people who become sleepy after several drinks would get sleepy after using marijuana. The comparison breaks down, however, because marijuana users almost always use marijuana sparingly; two or three "drags" on a marijuana cigarette or pipe usually satisfy the desire. This is no doubt due to the calming, rather than stimulating, results. Novices seeking "thrills" are tempted to overindulge, just as the same types would be excessive in their urge for "kicks" in other fields.

For the most part, the drug is cheaper and easier to find in Vietnam than a package of Lucky Strikes. It might be interesting to find out if the derivation of the R. J. Reynolds Tobacco Company's slogan "I'd walk a mile for a Camel" might not have come from the revered Arab expression "A puff of kif [hashish] in the morning makes a man as strong as a hundred camels in the courtyard."

Though the cities are full of the product, the deeper one goes into the countryside the more prevalent this strange member of the tea family becomes. For the American, it is very unlike the stateside atmosphere surrounding the drug. There is no central market for it in Vietnam. It is simply a way of life. One has merely to stumble on his way outside an American billet to bump into a man who might be selling the plant. Or he may take a deep breath anywhere to smell its dusty aroma. It is the slightest of achievements for an American to "score" on more marijuana than he has ever seen in his life. "Score," indeed. Who is it but the hotel maid or that friendly cyclo-driver who has been smoking it all this time, but the soldier didn't know it. When the realization finally strikes home (his attention having been otherwise diverted by the fact that each day may be his last), the average soldier sees that for all intents and purposes the entire country is stoned. For the kid who has spent the last few years of his life going through much shoe leather and money in trying to locate marijuana, Vietnam is that huge garden he has always dreamed about. And to think the Army sent him there!

The question comes up, "How many Americans in Vietnam smoke this ancient weed, and why, and when?" The answers, in that order, are that many (seventy-five per cent?) young soldiers smoke it, for all sorts of reasons, very often. This is a very hard statement to prove without actually asking men to admit to what their mother country maintains is a crime. However, some of the sociological backgrounds for this may help to explain these vast numbers [see Appendix I].

Much furor comes up from time to time about the number of Negro soldiers serving in Vietnam. My purpose is not to comment on what truth there might be in the allegation that there are too many, in proportion to their percentage of our population. Nor on the educational background of black GI's. Nor on their draft status because of that educational background. Nor on their numbers on the front line and in combat, because of the lack of any other skills. Neither is it my purpose to discuss here just why they might not have had a proper educational background and the skills in the first place. It is my purpose, however, to make the obvious statement that they brought their personal joys and sorrows with them. Added to that they brought the implements, effects, and customs of what, for the most part, might have been a predominantly slum environment, by the white soldier's standards. As any narcotics agent or *Time-Life* editor will tell you when not asked, the original marijuana traffic in America came out of the same part of town the colored boys have been caught in all their lives. Despite the fact that African *dagga* (hashish) came over with slavery, the black soldiers' predilection for "boo" (marijuana) is far more a matter of metropolitan geography than it is of color. If you can accept the facts already given, it is no huge feat of imagination to realize the particular joy received in the smoking of marijuana has no stigma whatsoever while serving what might be their last moments in the land of limitless "boo."

The colored soldier's brother-in-arms is the white draftee. They have more in common than one might think. The numerous reports of changing morals on the campus, and throughout the country, give a hint of the moral, or at least the smoking, fiber of upward of sixty per cent of America's educated youth. In fact, a Columbia University physician has said, " . . . if a male goes through four years of college on many campuses now without the [marijuana] experience, this abstinence bespeaks a rigidity in his character structure and fear of his impulses that is hardly desirable." Roughly the same percentage (sixty per cent) of GI's between the ages of eighteen and twenty-eight smoke, or have smoked, marijuana. And, of course, habits spread in the same way in the Army that they do in any blood fraternity. Add to that the fact that it's a hundred per cent easier to get marijuana in Vietnam than on a stateside campus (where it's very easy). This is not to say all who have smoked marijuana in Vietnam will continue to smoke it. A user might easily enjoy it but still become bored with or indifferent to its effects, just as many of the young Vietnamese do after a while.

Until recently, practically no civil or military controls were used in Vietnam to inhibit the smoking of marijuana, and it's doubtful the current furor will be very thorough or long-lasting. This is not so much a matter of kindly indulgence, though. It's simply that with all its other problems, the military has neither time nor inclination to try to jail such a huge part of its fighting force by stomping on marijuana. To enforce a prohibition against smoking the plant would be like trying to prohibit the inhalation of smog in Los Angeles. The military does not take as provincial a view of marijuana as American civilian law-enforcement agencies do. In a reception room of a rest and recuperation center at Camp Zama, Tokyo, an Army captain offers to return all drugs to soldiers on their return to Vietnam. If they aren't turned in, he advises the servicemen to keep them off their person while on the five-day stay in Japan. He says the girls in the Japanese bars which surround the Army post are given more or less a bounty by the Japanese police for every soldier they turn in for possessing drugs. Again he offers to return all drugs and any explosives when the soldiers depart for Vietnam. To the best of my knowledge, the captain was true to his word when we left. (Pharmacists in the port of Hong Kong, another R & R center, sell all manner of barbiturates, amphetamines, and other prescriptive drugs to military personnel without a prescription.)

The possession or use of narcotics is against Army regulations and is punishable under the Uniform Code of Military Justice. But as long as a soldier follows orders and performs his job, he rarely has problems with the establishment. Marijuana does not seem to get in the way of either of these two mainstays of military order. In fact, marijuana does not seem to get in the way of anything except ignorance about marijuana.

Finances pose no problem for the troops in Vietnam who wish to buy the plant. First of all there is often nothing else for the bulk of the front-line troops to buy. It's up to the local commanding officer, but the majority of "upcountry" PX's will sell liquor only to staff sergeants and up. This means a twenty-six-year-old corporal may not buy and drink what a nineteen-year-old sergeant may. It is possible to use marijuana for the entire twelve-month tour in Vietnam for about fifteen dollars. If you become friends with a farmer or mountain tribesman, there is no charge at all. But even though the availability of marijuana is so wide open, it is almost impossible for the most worldly city-minded newcomer to believe that marijuana is *all over* the place. The memory of America and its controls is hard to erase.

The first time I left Saigon for an extended period, for example, I took a knapsackful with me, thinking I would have to go back to Saigon to get more when my unit had smoked it all up. Though we hoarded it among us, supposing we had something nobody else had, we finally ran out after a few months of isolation atop Vung Chau Mountain. When the supply ran out, I was sent on a mercy mission to the local village.

I used the laundry at the bottom of the mountain as my base camp for the search-and-clear operation I had been charged with by my fellow soldiers. The laundry, which was really just a village home, was owned by a wonderful drunken Vietnamese ex-soldier. He never did anything but laugh, and constantly hug us, his children, and his wife—as she did all of our laundry in their back yard. In payment for this constant good cheer and friendship, we would buy him beer at the PX in town. In payment for that, he would find the cleanest girls in the area to help share this beautiful circle of international good will. We loved him and traditionally called him Papa-san. Papa-san hated our first sergeant, who constantly bitched about the laundry because Mrs. Papa-san did such an awful job, but Papa-san's feelings about the sergeant, in turn, erased our misgivings about the laundry and only served to enhance our love for his dear family and its many services to us. Our unit was the first group of GI's he had ever had any close contact with.

On my search, I spent whatever time I could find for days babbling and making smoking gestures at the people in the countryside, rolling my eyes to overstate my quest. At first they would seem confused, but then slowly, very slowly, an idea would crystallize and they would run off with unbounded insight in their hearts. Invariably they came back with American cigarettes stolen from the PX. On some occasions it would be a pipe, or a Havana cigar, but always with that look of self-satisfaction which comes from complete understanding. After many such incidents, I finally became totally depressed with my inability to communicate with the peasants and went back to Papa-san's to get drunk. He saw the state I was in and offered me his bed to lie in to help ease my burden. He seemed very distracted with my ill humor and discreetly left the little room while I searched my mind for feasible excuses to get me back to Saigon for a day.

About at the point where I had decided that I needed a new life-insurance policy—a piece of paperwork that could only be done in Saigon—Papa-san apologetically knocked on the door and meekly entered the room offering something that, if I tried it, might make things a little better. He had lit a pipe, and before he got ten feet away, I knew what was in it. I had just spent days going all over Qui Nhon, and here stood Papa-san, the main distributor of processed marijuana for practically the entire province. He thought we liked beer.

You may now have a picture of the American fighting machine composed mostly of a group of youngsters enjoying the not-so-secret rites of *Cannabis*. This is not far wrong, because the mass use of some kind of drug in war is as ancient as war itself. The early Greek historian Herodotus described how the Scythians laid hemp on hot stones and then breathed in the fumes which would arise. This practice was indulged in both before and after battle, so it would be difficult to conclude that the experience was solely for the purpose of inciting to violence. The Vikings well knew the mind-expanding *Amanita* mushrooms (those brilliantly red-spotted ones featured in a section of Walt Disney's *Fantasia*) and they would eat the fungus before battle for its mixture of both inner calm and energy. The Viking ritual included being dressed up in a bearskin after which appropriate ceremonies and incantations took place in an effort to whip up emotion. The word "berserk" comes from the Nordic language and was used to describe the state of enthusiasm achieved by the bearskin-clad warriors. This is like the word "panic" used by the ancient Greeks, who in worshipping the goat-footed god Pan would partake of organic mind drugs along with their wine. Homer makes numerous references to "nepenthe" and describes it as a drug that was put in the wine which would "lull all pain and anger, and bring forgetfulness of every sorrow." Homer makes it clear that anyone who partook was in no way incapacitated but, on the contrary, was better equipped to cope with either joy or sorrow. It is uncertain just what "nepenthe" was extracted from except that it is described as a naturally growing wild plant.

It is extremely important to bear in mind that marijuana definitely does not cause violence. [After this article was published, many people wrote to me apparently unable to understand this point because they concluded that I meant to tell them their sons were being doped into some kind of maniac fighters, by a conspiracy of the Viet Cong and the naïveté of the Army in allowing this to happen.] I don't think that marijuana always produces noticeable alterations in the mind. But in certain situations, such as just before a battle, almost anything eaten, smoked, or imbibed in any fashion assumes a kind of sacrament. If used as a sacrament, Skippy peanut butter could produce enthusiasm and group spirit. And I've heard soldiers fantasizing about peanut butter and wishing they could suddenly have a jar materialize in their hands. Just by itself this kind of mind drug allows a certain amount of mental flexibility, and an almost spiritual easiness that can lead either to lethargy or excitement. Suffice it to say that these drugs, including marijuana, bring a sort of mildly ethereal happiness, and what acts are to be performed within the gates of this happiness are up to the individual and the situation. Marijuana for the most part leads to a calm, perspective detachment [see Appendix I].

Because of what marijuana does to the brain's interpretation of light, and what we call beauty, a wonderful change in war can occur, just as eating chocolate helps to fight a war also, and chocolate is included in the rations. After smoking marijuana, explosions modulate musically instead of being heard in grim terror. Death takes on a new, approachable symbolism that is not so horrible. All the senses, including the emotions, may seem muted by being hypercharged with their own capacity. There is not enough time to delve into the unusual manifestations of fear with this entirely new lexicon of sights and thoughts to deal with. And the changes keep occurring. I well remember sitting on top of a bunker with about twenty friends during what we thought to be a surprise attack on our mountain. It was about midnight. The South China Sea was behind us with an opaque moon spreading its glory out over the mixture of Navy ships and sampans in the harbor a mile below us in Qui Nhon. Their lights seemed to twinkle back recognition of our appreciation. Many an Oriental artist has tried to capture just such a scene. In front of us, in the direction of the supposed attack, lay the beautiful mountains and valleys of the central highlands. The blue-green rolling hills were studded here and there with volcanic boulders that shouted their blackness back at the stoned eyes that beheld them in the delicate moonlight. When the flares and fifty-caliber machine guns started up for cover, you could barely hear the noise of the ordnance over the ohs and ahs coming from our little group of defenders, smoking Papa-san's marijuana. The beauty of all that gunpowder (an Oriental invention, remember) was almost too much to bear. Up would shoot a white star flare on a parachute, and all eyes would be transfixed by the glow. Of course it was intended to show whether the enemy was coming up our side of the crest, but a sigh of "did you dig that?" whispered past the shuffling of grenades and ammunition. The mutual feeling was, "If this is it, what a nice way to go." The clatter of the machine guns was like a Stravinsky percussion interlude from *Le Sacre du Printemps*. Later we found out what we had suspected, that there was no attack, but it was a "good show." There isn't a psychedelic discothèque that can match the beauty of flares and bombs at night.

Everyone in our group was left with the feeling we were unique in this war to be seeing it from such a detached and aesthetic vantage point. That was until discussion started up on the mountain after it was all over. Other GI's, when commenting on the action, or any action, would say, "Yeah, but you should see it when you're high." To have this social ploy stolen away by a meager infantry type (we were radio and television specialists) seemed a great shame, until further investigation proved virtually everyone was smoking marijuana before, during, and after the shooting. Not just on my mountain. Not just in my bunker, but on every mountain and in every bunker in Vietnam by both sides. Under the pressure of war, everyone seeks release from it. Perhaps for many GI's, smoking marijuana was the only, and sometimes final, relief that Vietnam had to offer. Sometimes you would hear friends of a dead soldier say, "At least he was stoned."

The mountainous country surrounding Dien Bien Phu has traditionally been the largest opium-producing district in all of what was Indochina. For centuries the opium poppies have been milked by the mountain tribesmen who maintain the fields for the usual reasons. More recently, the proceeds from this natural drug were used by the Viet Minh to help finance their war against France. The raw opium was sold through the markets of the Orient to buy arms, and there is no reason not to assume the practice still goes on under the auspices of the National Liberation Front. Of course, today pretty bombs and flares and tracers come as gifts from sympathetic pyrotechnical supply houses such as the Soviet Union and Communist China, though it can safely be assumed opium is still a supplemental source of income for the National Liberation Front. As I said before, an addictive drug is not the best thing to ingest when heavy exercise, such as shooting at people, is anticipated.

Opium is a drug for old men in this part of Asia, and wealthy old men at that. I had a good friend, a North Vietnamese, in Saigon, who went heavily into debt after his father's funeral. There was an elaborate funeral ceremony and a suitable period afterward for mourning. Many of his father's elderly friends and other older relatives came to Hanoi for this entire period, and they had to be given board and room and opium as honored guests. My friend went broke in the process, and although he understood the necessity for this hospitality, it was a difficult time for him.

However, it is very true that marijuana is used extensively, not specifically for the purpose of war, but as a way of life. It is a sad coincidence that so many people in Southeast Asia have seen nothing but war; beyond this, marijuana and war should not be connected.

Betel (used so commonly in South America) is chewed by the majority of the peoples of Southeast Asia. It is one of nature's stimulants. It is more common in North and South Vietnam, and used more extensively than tobacco is in the rest of the world. The mixture of nut, leaf, and lime that makes up the betel morsel causes the teeth to turn black and everything else in the mouth to turn reddish-orange. Though the Vietnamese don't really enjoy having reddish-orange mouths, they do enjoy the "pep" or the "buzz" that betel gives them. The chewing of the fruit of this palm gives the chewer quick energy, a sense of well-being, and calmness. It also gives him stamina and endurance. It becomes obvious that some of America's favorite drugs serve exactly the same functions.

In moments of contemplation in Vietnam, I began to wonder where the "mysterious Oriental" had gone. Oh, the silliness of the name-calling that was needed just to keep up suspicion and fear on both sides. As in all the wars before it, the opposing side *had* to be barbarians of a sort, and if they were not . . . why fight? Where to find the personal animosity to fire wars? It seemed that political arguments would not be able to survive their own stupidity without first building the adversary into a fiend of some sort. Once this was accomplished, a man-to-man personal hatred was engendered and this could keep a war going for centuries, and of course it has done just that.

It has been well reported that Viet Cong and North Vietnamese troops use drugs in battle. These reports seem to have been designed to give them a sinister image of zombies or robots for a political machine that keeps them drugged to fulfill that government's evil intentions, and keeps them slaves to the system. Anyone familiar with marijuana would have to laugh at this concept.

Clearly there is very little difference between the state of mind of the stoned Viet Cong and the stoned GI. The dead Viet Cong found with drugs on his person resembles in every way the dead American found with drugs. For that matter they both resemble the dead suburban commuter who is killed in an automobile accident in the U.S. and is found with some pills on his person—as he is very apt to be found. If the GI also has his survival kit with him containing all those dextro-amphetamines, who looks worse? And whose hermetically sealed government is supplying whom? With what? And why? If we investigate sources thoroughly it is very likely we would find the Communist got his little bag of marijuana from his wife before he left the tunnel that morning.

The Viet Cong sometimes wields a small musical instrument called a bugle. He may even be tempted to toot it as he runs along. The Allied mind finds this practice sinister. We don't seem repelled by the Scottish bagpipes or the thrill of a rebel yell. After all, any child knows that he can relax when the cavalry starts sounding off—and yet, down on our imagination comes a fanatic band of "junkie" Orientals with black pajamas on, slit eyes, and reddish-orange mouths, howling like wolves with strange bugles blaring. What hath God wrought? From a purely public-relations standpoint, it would be interesting to see what Americans would have done to besmear the ancient Britons who had the nerve to paint themselves blue for combat. For that matter, I wonder what the ancient Britons would have thought of an American Army sergeant climbing on a troop plane in Pleiku with six human ears wired to his belt. I wonder if he would stop to consider the sergeant's "civilized" motives before he filed *his* tribal press release.

To take this line of reasoning to the extreme, the chains that have been found binding Viet Cong gunners to their weapons serve a very basic psychological purpose when washed with the same intellectual detergent we use about napalm and gas in Vietnam. Once a man knows he has no other way out than victory, he can devote all his attention to that end. The Viet Cong sometimes bind *themselves* with chains as a gesture of determination for their comrades, a gesture not unlike the signature on a marriage contract or the death penalty for desertion and cowardice that can be enforced under the United States Army's Uniform Code of Military Justice. (I wish I knew the translation for "We have not yet begun to fight" in Vietnamese.) Congress will give a man's wife a medal because he threw himself on a hand grenade to save the lives of the men in his squad. If it had been a Viet Cong, it probably would be reported as an act of fanaticism by an individual probably hypnotized with drugs, or with fear of reprisals on his family, or just everyday Oriental suicide. If the American and Communist soldiers are *both* taking drugs as they face each other for the kill, could this be any stranger than if they weren't?

The two armies may well be sent out to dance to a ghastly libretto composed by government leaders and officials all suffering from quite a different "high" of their own. The quality of *that* "high" is one that neither of these two combatants could begin to guess at . . . straight, or stoned, themselves.

The scenario is what they call modern warfare, guerrilla warfare, pacification, liberation, oppression, suppression, repression—or perhaps self-deception. Deception to the point that the cogs on both sides have retreated by smoking or chewing their happiness in the face of it all.

Many nights I would just lie quietly on some sandbags, trying to sort it all out. The quality of this kind of search is no different whether it be in a presidential rocking chair or in a foxhole. I was very happy that because of a few plants, Americans and Viet Cong alike didn't have to bear the naked weight of other people's decisions and foregone conclusions. At least they had the buffer of their mind—its happiness, its desires, its woes—those textures which would always remain untouched by leaflets or campaign speeches, or bullets, or horror. This part of the mind was in itself an area of peace into which no one might trespass: a hallowed garden of thought which could be maintained even in the face of all calamity. I would play a game in my head which I will pass on to people in a less picturesque setting. It was a game of bitter equations.

I began by picturing armies at their game on opposing sides of a table. The fact that there was a game at all was supported by their suspicions and affirmations about each other. I couldn't believe the feelings, beliefs, and motivations of the Viet Cong were less pure than ours just because of their proximity to the table. To the Vietnamese, the particular shape of their humanity, their way of life, is no more or less immoral or atrocious than the American feels his to be. The game progresses, and the game gets worse. There is no final score kept on the table other than what can be measured in mutual loss. (Once it has become isolated into a game for contemplation on a mountaintop it is a little distracting to keep being reminded by the clothes you are wearing that you cannot play the game at all without assuming there is a right and a wrong side of the table.)

Now picture the entire tableful of men, each hidden in the playings of his own mind by the effect of this strange plant. Not one of them is really very involved with the table at all. They all seem to be acting out someone else's conviction, someone else's hatred. Look closely and see if it isn't yours.

There is, monks, an unborn, not become, not made, uncompounded, and were it not, monks, for this unborn, not become, not made, uncompounded, no escape could be shown here for what is born, has become, is made, is compounded. But, because there is, monks, an unborn, not become, not made, uncompounded, therefore an escape can be shown for what is born, has become, is made, is compounded, and were it not, monks, for this . . .

IV

I hadn't seen Thom since I'd left for Vietnam, and so I had
a lot to fill him in on. He had enlisted in the Army to beat
the draft and had been around to various posts for training
during the year since he enlisted. He had heard a lot about
Vietnam through conversations with other Army personnel
who had come back. We swapped stories about Vietnam in
general but mostly about marijuana. Thom and I had both
become acquainted with marijuana at about the same time
in our early youth in New York City. We had tried it once
or twice at parties with friends of ours. It wasn't until I got
to Vietnam that I came across the use of marijuana in any
great quantities. When I was growing up in New York the
places where my friends would have to go to get marijuana
were generally some of the most unpleasant imaginable. This
was partly due to the fact that all big cities do have slum
areas where marijuana is used, but it was also due to the
fact that ordinary young people hadn't become involved with
marijuana as they have in recent years. In those days (actually, since the original marijuana laws in the 1930's) mu-
sicians were about the only people in the news who were
associated with smoking the drug. As the years went by and
marijuana became popular on college campuses, the students
began to do their own dealing and growing and buying and
selling, to lower the prices and keep their business away from
the Mafia underworld.

I was a little nervous on the drive to New York about meeting my father. I wasn't so much worried about his attitude about the marijuana offense itself as I was regretful of and sympathetic to the situation I'd put him in with regard to his friends. I recalled my father talking about marijuana from time to time, if the subject ever came up, and he had a fairly complete knowledge of its effect. I was sure that in his mind there was no feeling of "my son, the junkie." But of course in the minds of most parents today, the problem with marijuana is not so much any insurmountable obstacle in communications with their children about the drug itself so much as it is the laws regarding marijuana. Parents seem to have learned from all the magazine and newspaper articles about it that marijuana is very likely not as bad for one's health as cigarettes, but parents do not want their children's pictures in the paper attached to an item about being arrested for marijuana usage. Never mind about the health aspect.

Thom had been in the Army then less than a year and he was still trying to accommodate himself to the complex Army discipline routines when so much of it seemed absurd. Like anyone in the Army these days he was trying to give his life some kind of meaning and reality, and this is of course impossible for anyone who is—as he was—going to be sent to Vietnam soon. When we were growing up together he and I would have shared many of the same strains and pangs of growing up and we would have shared the feeling that these things only became difficult when juxtaposed to parents. Therefore, although in many ways our lives have gone off in different directions, we had a common bond within the family relationship. I was just about through it all as far as the Army was concerned. If I didn't stumble into a court-martial I would be discharged in December. Thom still had two years facing him and he didn't quite see how he would make it sometimes. Even though I had less than a hundred days to serve I was beginning to wonder if I'd make it.

Thom asked me how I thought Dad had reacted to all my

problems of the last few days. I said that Dad was probably going to be very good about it. In times of family crisis he was always very good. I remember one time when I'd been kicked out of summer school for cheating on a French test. The next thing I knew, I was on a bus headed for New York and my father met me at the bus station. He joked a bit and related similar lapses in character from his own youth in order to make me feel a little bit more relaxed about it, and slowly, very slowly, we could reconstruct where I'd gone wrong. In the end I would feel chastened, but whatever might have been tragic would have come to seem silly. His reaction to the marijuana arrest would be pretty much the same except for one difference. As far as cheating was concerned I would have felt that I definitely had erred. But as for marijuana I didn't think I'd gone wrong. I'd just been caught. Somewhere in here is the basis for the credibility gap between many parents and their children about marijuana. The parents would like the children to say I'm wrong and I'll take my medicine, rather than say I'm not wrong and take that medicine away. This seems particularly relevant because the laws against marijuana seem like medicine which is prescribed for an illness that doesn't exist in the belief of the patient. There was no question in my mind about the fact that there were going to be problems between my father and myself, but the problems would be felt rather than spoken about. On the surface, things would be just as pleasant as our combined good taste could possibly preserve, but there would be no real hiding the displeasure this time. And there would be no regarding this as a boyish prank and "don't do it again." This was mainly because I wouldn't feel it would be wrong to do it again.

We drove until late at night and arrived in the city about two a.m. It was the first time in about four years my stepmother had seen my brother. Thom and I had been living in California for several years before we went into the Army, and it was Thom's first time back in New York. There was a note from my stepmother to wake her up when we arrived, and so we did. There were many hugs, and "are-you-all-right?" and "you-look-so-good!" Then quickly we got to the point that had been bothering my parents ever since their lawyer had reported I didn't want his services because I already had a lawyer. There was no doubt my parents would have preferred that I use their lawyer. And when I didn't they were worried that I had fallen into the clutches of some fast-talking, crooked type who had an office over a pawnshop and preyed on young people in trouble. When it turned out that my lawyer was a highly respected Georgetown attorney they worried that he was probably very expensive and out to make a reputation with marijuana decisions and was going to use the family name to promote the enterprise. I did my best to make it clear this was not the case, but I also knew if they wanted to think the worst they would reap the worst by having to endure their own imagination.

I had sent my father a manuscript copy of the *Washingtonian* article about the use of marijuana in Vietnam, and when we arrived at the hospital the next day I gave him a string of hippie beads Fralich had left on the dashboard of the car to make father feel fully initiated into the fraternity. I found my father lying in bed wearing a T-shirt with a picture of W. C. Fields airbrushed on the front. On the bridge of his reading glasses was perched a stuffed canary which peered down into the pages of the book he was reading. He commented that the bird had stopped on his way south for a bite of tasty hospital food. Many of his friends had brought presents, like the T-shirt, which reflected his very pixielike personality. There was a large poster that said "SMOKE PEANUT BUTTER, NOT POT." I added my Army News Feature display to the decor. He hadn't yet been operated on and he was decked out in a counterweight device that was designed to stretch his spine. He seemed to love the mechanics of the thing and was continually altering the tension, just to play with it. He was glad to see me but there was a definite strain in coming face to face with me for the first time since he had seen me three days earlier on TV when I was arrested.

It was the first time my father had seen Thom since he'd moved to California. I'd been stationed in D.C. for three months and had been able to drive up to visit him fairly often. Thom and he had a lot of lies to swap. Underlying all the jokes, though, were always passing remarks about the fact that I was going to be the first credentialed felon of the tribe. When the conversation shifted more seriously to my arrest, my father was mainly concerned about my relationship with the Army because of the arrest and also because of the statements I'd been making about the use of marijuana in Vietnam. Since he had been a correspondent in World War II he was very sensitive to the retaliation which would surely result when the military image was injured. There was no need to be anything but candid, so I told him exactly what I thought was happening in the more and more congested public-relations lobe of the official Army mind where young Steinbeck was concerned.

I had been drafted just like anybody else, but my specialty was in Information, since I'd been working as a radio and TV announcer and reporter before I was drafted. This background fitted right into the modern concept of the Army controlling its own information about itself as well as the information it distributes to the public. Now, after a fairly patriotic career, it looked like I was stabbing my own department right in the back. The office where I worked in Washington was the same office which would eventually have to publish all the lists of facts and figures necessary to convince the civilians what I was saying about marijuana wasn't true. In a way, it was only because I was *so* ripe for a court-martial that the Army was kept from going through with it. To punish me would only bring it all out in the open even more, and would hurt the Army as much as to say I was right. They hated the image of themselves as being quick to silence any protest, but this was the image they themselves had made and thus they were paralyzed by it all. It would be one thing if some private from Peoria had said that the young GI's in Vietnam were turning on with marijuana. That private

E

would have disappeared into Leavenworth in a flash. But here I was; the son of "the conscience of America." How could they banish me quietly? My father mumbled something into his beard at that.

On the drive to New York I had heard a taped news statement of General Westmoreland saying my entire story about marijuana was ridiculous. I was a little surprised to think a four-star general would get himself into the position of bothering to contradict a specialist fourth class who was still on active duty. But it was a revealing lesson about how seriously the Army takes its public image. The Army was trapped, apparently. When I had been arrested I was told that the Information Office had cleared me, and I was free to talk to reporters. Naturally, the Army public-relations officers thought I would have to answer questions about my arrest. My article wasn't going to be published until after I was out of the Army, so they didn't have *that* to worry about. However, they had not fully digested the work of the narcotics agents.

When Ian Fralich was arrested the narcotics agents took a manuscript copy of my article and went out of their way to quote parts of it to news reporters at the time in an effort to defend their position as clever sleuths and ready to respond on any matter of drug abuse. This had been picked up by the wire services and given worldwide coverage. Therefore, when the reporters got to me after the Army clearance, they were anxious to fire direct questions about the use of marijuana in Vietnam. The rule in the Army was that no piece could appear in a civilian publication without having first been cleared by the Information Office. That office was certainly not about to clear my article, so I was content to wait until I was out of the Army rather than be court-martialed for *breaking a rule,* no matter what I might say on any subject in the article. The first comments I made had led to Westmoreland's denial. The clearance was immediately revoked after that and I was ordered not to make any statement about any aspect of Vietnam without specific clearance from the Information Office. Furthermore, I was ordered not to discuss the fact with anyone that I had been so ordered.

It looked as if there was nothing for the Army to do but shut me up as best they could without making too much fuss about it. All they could do was wait and see if I was judged innocent or guilty in the civil trial. Though possession of marijuana is an easy court-martial conviction in the service, the Army had no case against me. The marijuana was not found in a government barracks, but in my apartment. Everyone in the Army's Information section lived in civilian quarters. I told my father I was going to have my trial postponed until after I was out of the Army. Thus the Army would have to discharge me or hold me, and it would be awkward for them if they held me. It would seem as if they were trying to put me in jail for what I said rather than anything else. If I were given a not-guilty verdict the Army could build a case against me only with the same evidence that produced the not-guilty verdict in open court. Or they could let me go. They couldn't change the comments that I had already made because they had given me the clearance. If I were given a guilty verdict the civilian authorities would have charge of me and the Army would have no part to play. All the Army had left was to court-martial me for being an embarrassment to the military, which would be as good as saying I was right in my statements about Vietnam, which would be a real embarrassment.

My father's response to all this was mixed. He tended to doubt everything was as inexorable as I said it was but he was amused that all the Army self-consciousness had come back to cut its own throat. Our conversation turned to the *Washingtonian* article. My father has always been interested in other people's cultures and we talked for some time about the Vietnamese. He complimented me on some of the descriptive passages and he corrected me on a few minor facts about the use of drugs by the Greeks and then he got to the point which was troubling him. He said that many of his friends who were reporters in Vietnam didn't share my opinion at all that marijuana was used by so many servicemen there. In fact, one friend of his said more marijuana was used by the press corps in Vietnam than anyone else. He was concerned that I would be stepped on and contradicted or made a fool of because of the seventy-five per cent figure everyone wanted to pick up on. I told him my purpose in writing the piece was not to search for sensationalism so much as to dramatize the vast numbers of Americans who were smoking marijuana in Vietnam, and if they were smoking it as respected and lauded soldiers over there how could it be they were criminals in America? What I wanted to do most of all was paint this ridiculous contradiction in a setting where contradictions cannot be reduced to a simple statement (droning through the United States) that, well, the laws are wrong but we've got to live with them.

With Americans dying by the hundreds each week in Vietnam, it seemed to me that if people could be confronted with the juxtaposition they would recognize this ridiculous aspect and would be stimulated to some new thinking on the subject. Father began to question my ethics: was I using figures I knew weren't true? It was all well and good to illustrate a statement about contradicting moralities, but if I was beginning to be a writer was it good to make inaccurate statements when I was asking to be read for accuracy? Crusading may be fine for Ralph Nader, but if I was to be taken seriously as a writer perhaps a more contained approach would be better, even when I was convinced that my cause was just. We discussed this at length and he did agree with me that no precise statistics would be available now, or ever, on the subject of marijuana use in Vietnam any more than such figures are available for marijuana use in the United States. He still insisted it would be wiser to discuss marijuana using facts and figures which would be more digestible and believable to the majority of readers. I told him I was not concerned whether the figures were correct to fifteen per cent or even twenty per cent; the results of my investigations on the subject led me to believe that over half the American land-based troops in Vietnam between the ages of nineteen and twenty-seven were smoking marijuana. And if they weren't smoking it when I was there to the tune of seventy-five per cent, it could only be a matter of months before the trend caught up with the figures and perhaps went beyond them. In the end one would have to be persuaded by subjective judgments, just as one is as to whether the Americans are winning the war in Vietnam or not, despite the statistics to support the pros or cons of the issue.

I explained also that I thought the Department of Defense's reaction to my statements were something that I could weigh very delicately since I had worked in the Army Information Office which was generating and releasing those statements. I believed that if marijuana in Vietnam wasn't a reality for the American reader now, by the time the Department of Defense got through denying its use in the military it would be a reality. The Department of Defense's little incremental facts and figures, statistics that were brought up to deny my statistics, would leave a vacuum for their own doubt. How could the Army be sure their 509 reported users of marijuana represented anything except a meaningless sample? Since it is forbidden to smoke marijuana, what soldier is going to admit it to an investigator? Until marijuana is made legal no true figures can even be hoped for and by that time no one will care about figures. The number of users reported on a university campus or at a military academy are similarly bound to be inaccurate. During the recent scandal at Annapolis there was official admission of three or four users among the midshipmen during the first stages of the publicity. Gradually the figures mounted and finally dozens were expelled. Surely nobody can believe the final figure (which was released to the public as well over a hundred who were expelled) represented the total number of boys who had used marijuana.

The same thing happened when I was in the Army at San Francisco and marijuana use came in for a round of publicity at the Treasure Island station. Likewise, when the figures are released to show the amount of marijuana confiscated at the

Mexican border, can anyone really know whether those figures represent ten per cent, or ninety per cent of the amount of marijuana which is actually being smuggled into the country? It seemed to me that the Army and I would both be caught for a time in the limbo of incredibility. In time the fact would be believed that marijuana was being used in Vietnam in incredibly large amounts by an equally incredibly large number of American servicemen. Once my statement was published newsmen would make a big effort to check out the marijuana situation in Vietnam. They might have to look a little further than they had looked but not very much further. Since I planned to return to Vietnam maybe I could help them with hints: cool, lukewarm, warm, warmer . . . My father seemed to realize this was my final opinion of the ethics of the piece and the accuracy of it and we concluded the conversation with his giving me the tremendous compliment of saying he thought it was well written no matter what it said and whether or not he agreed with the approach I was using. It was clear to him that within the article I was trying to make a deeply personal statement about war, as well as marijuana, and the release from the confusion of being aware that you may die soon.

The weekend went quickly, and as I said goodbye I felt that my parents understood that I didn't want them to be technically involved with my trial. They asked me to keep in touch with them, and wished me luck.

V

When I got back to Washington the next morning, I received a message saying that General Ware, the Chief of the Army Information Service, had been trying to find me late Friday, after I had left for New York. It was obviously in reaction to the fact that the military command in Vietnam had laid itself on the line by condescending to contradict a specialist fourth class. I have no idea what the interview with General Ware would have been like had I happened to have been in town when he called. Though I waited all day Monday expecting a summons to his office, it never came, and I heard nothing more from any Army officials. Perhaps the Army relaxed, or retreated into a philosophy the officials often use—if the problem is left alone, maybe it won't rear its head again. I began to feel a bit intoxicated with power; I may have been able to intimidate the Army a trifle instead of becoming the more classic victim. It crossed my mind to start formal procedures to clear my article with the Army before I left the service so that it might be published while I was still in uniform. But I knew they'd never clear it. I speculated about what overcompensating reactions they might have to the article that would again end up with the same effect as affirming it. But finally this seemed too much and I got control of my growing sense of mischief in dealing with my colleagues. I would have my day and it would be as a civilian not as a soldier. The article was due to be published in the

January issue of *The Washingtonian* and it was fast coming up Pearl Harbor Day, which was the end of my enlistment. All that I had in front of me now was the trial and the psychological squeeze of twenty-three year-long days until I was out.

As the days went by Lowe and I began to prepare the defense for my case. My plea had been not guilty and grounds for the defense would be partly based on the fact that I had written articles on the subject of marijuana in Vietnam and I was around the hippies to study the marijuana phenomenon since my interest had been piqued by its use in Vietnam. It is particularly difficult to write about my motivations and intentions during the period of my trial. Since the first session I had with Agents Parnetta and MacKinnon I had found myself increasingly serious about trying to stir up some new thinking about marijuana. It was not exactly a mission but on that order. However, a courtroom is no place for a defendant to appear as a missionary. I felt somewhat schizo during the proceedings but maybe that is also part of my natural personality, because it was definitely me that the jury found not guilty. It is impossible for me to give an objective or a narrative account of that trial because I think any trial is intensely subjective in the first place. Nevertheless, by this time I had become a writer for the *Washingtonian* and because my trial was newsworthy for several reasons the magazine decided to follow up the article on Vietnam with another relating to the trial. Another writer, Tom Kelly, who is a friend of mine and also an expert at making trial transcripts come to life, was charged with the assignment. I was asked to do an article which would be coupled with his and would provide the preliminary details. Those details have now become the bulk of this book instead because right after the trial I found myself unable to write about any part of it and much involved in writing several other articles instead. Kelly ended up doing the whole thing, and I think his piece is without a doubt more perceptive of the court and the entire situation than anything I could write because of my own role in it. He has given his permission to include it here. Although the beginning of Kelly's article covers in brief some of what I've already written here, his particular view of those same circumstances puts them in different perspective. In the dead seriousness of the trial, from where I sat, there was no way for me to see the somewhat commonplace struggle of the two generations trying to defend and give precedents for their respective beliefs and action using a common law and common logic.

"WHO ME? I'M A SOCIOLOGIST"

The strange things you have to do to get out of
trouble when your apartment is raided and found
to contain twenty pounds of marijuana and a
crowd of wretched hippies.

John Steinbeck IV is serious-minded, he has a trim beard,
and he is the son of the celebrated author of *Grapes of Wrath*.

He is twenty-one years old.

He is a rather startlingly good example of the generational
gap—some of his contemporaries regard a joint of marijuana
with the easy familiarity with which the generation of, say,
Detective Edmond MacKinnon of the narcotics squad regards a cup of tea.

The pot generation calls the kettle generation black and
the kettle boils over.

. . . One day last August Detective MacKinnon came to call.
It was their first meeting and the detective was looking for a
leak. He later testified that he had "made a raid on a premises
at 2151 K Street, N.W., known as The Source. It was owned
and operated by John Ian Fralich. When we arrived there
the place was empty. One man was there and greeted us at the
door and said, 'I knew you were coming,' and . . . he told me
that he received a call from Mr. Steinbeck. . . .

"We told him [Mr. Steinbeck] that when we raided the
place his name came up as being the one that called the
Source and informed them of our plans . . . Of course there
was nothing substantiated to this bit of information and the
main reason, like I say, for our going over to talk to Mr.
Steinbeck, was to find out who he was because it was just
another name in the leakage of the information of us with
our warrants."

Detective MacKinnon emphasized that he had not gone to the Pentagon to arrest Steinbeck or, indeed, to intimidate him. But some weeks later about one thirty in the afternoon of October 16, Detective MacKinnon and his partner, Detective Clyde Rice, dropped in on Steinbeck's apartment at 1737 F Street, N.W. Steinbeck wasn't home, but three hippies were: Ian Fralich, and two young ladies, Jean Lasar and Nancy Marnett. The officers had a warrant for Jean, who had just returned from New York. She was in bed, hippies being often late risers. When MacKinnon appeared she asked him to hand her her pants, meaning her dungarees, which she put on under the covers. The prospect of a young woman in bed in a young man's apartment probably seems more significant to the middle-aged than to the hip. The flower children have shucked off some of the conventions surrounding beds.

After Jean put her pants on, Detective MacKinnon opened a suitcase which was sitting in the middle of the floor and asked her if she knew what was in it. She said yes, twenty pounds of marijuana and it all belonged to her.

The detectives then seized evidence here and there and arrested Jean, Nancy, and Ian. Steinbeck, meanwhile, was back at the office tending to the nation's defense, more or less. When he returned that evening he found his home a shambles. . . .

He was charged with possession of narcotics, meaning marijuana, and with maintaining a nuisance, which can mean in the arcane language of the law, having a home at which narcotic users regularly gather. On December 18, in due process, the case came up before Judge Edmond T. Daly in the criminal division of the District of Columbia court of general sessions, with James Phelps, Esq., prosecuting and Ira M. Lowe, Esq., defending.

The law is a number of things, but it is not a member of any particular generation. It regards the elderly banker and the young hippie with the same dispassionate eye. The men who are the instruments of the law are not, of course, always so detached. With the best of intentions they may try to force the law to do something it is not meant to do. Indeed, it is assumed that a defense attorney will use every legitimate device to win acquittal. (He will not bribe a juror, but he will split a hair, exaggerate a point, or display violent emotion he does not feel.) Good judges, however, keep everybody in line.

A trial is a contest, but not a contest between the principals named in the charge. The United States of America was arraigned against John Steinbeck IV but neither had control over the machinery. James Phelps, the Assistant United States Attorney who handles the heavy majority of the narcotic prosecutions, and Ira Lowe, who has a particular feeling about marijuana laws, did. Judge Daly was both the man in charge and the man in the middle.

The case began to the advantage of the defense, with prosecutor Phelps announcing that he was dropping the charge alleging possession. That left only the charge that Steinbeck "maintained a nuisance."

"So there you have half the case, Mr. Lowe," the judge said amiably.

Mr. Lowe tried to get rid of the other half, asking that the nuisance charge be dropped on the grounds that marijuana is not a narcotic. "I know your Honor is not going to agree to that," he said. Lawyers often ask for things they are not going to get. They are, as they say, building a record. Prosecutor Phelps then announced the shape of his strategy. He would call four witnesses: the two detectives, Edmond MacKinnon and Clyde E. Rice, Steinbeck's landlady—to prove that he did really live at his address, and a government chemist, John Steele, who had examined the marijuana in the suitcase and found it to be, indeed marijuana. He said he would also show that in addition to the marijuana in the suitcase, the raiding detectives had seized "pipes, cigarette rollers, and the "like" and that these had contained "traces" of marijuana.

The "traces," interestingly, had not been found by chemist Steele but by another government chemist named

Milton Tannenbaum. Mr. Tannenbaum was not available to testify, but the defense had agreed that he had reported "traces," as it agreed with all the other observations made so far by Mr. Phelps. The "traces" would become the most fascinating point of the case. But the court had first to dispose of Mr. Lowe's contention that the whole matter should be dropped since marijuana is not, scientifically, a narcotic. The question of whether a thing can be one thing scientifically and another legally is the essence and the glory of the law. It is also the peculiarity that prompts some to call the law an ass. Mr. Lowe argued that marijuana is "not a narcotic . . . because it is not habit-forming, it is not addictive, it is not harmful to the body . . . It is more of a stimulant, and a narcotic is generally a depressant." He admitted that the law against "maintaining a nuisance" defined marijuana as a narcotic, but said that conviction under the law would be cruel and unusual punishment. Mr. Phelps replied simply that "Congress says it is, even if in fact it scientifically isn't." And by the rules of the game that resolved the matter.

One might wonder here at the significance of the semantics and the force of traditional attitudes. If marijuana was not generally considered a narcotic—and therefore akin to heroin, cocaine, and opium—would there be the vigorous pursuit of those, like Steinbeck, who have a certain partiality for it? In other words, what would happen if marijuana was outlawed, but not for the ugly reason that it's a narcotic?

Marijuana is considered a social lubricant in some cultures, as whiskey is in ours. Even when whiskey was outlawed, no one frowned particularly on a man who took an occasional belt. And would a prohibition agent have charged a man with possession after smelling the faint essence of bourbon in an empty shot glass?

The debaters then moved to the subject of "traces."

"Traces" of marijuana—specks too small to be weighed on the usual sensitive scale—cannot be used as evidence to convict anyone of possession.

The prosecution had already abandoned its attempt to

convict Steinbeck of possession.

But Mr. Phelps, in a tangle of language and logic, tried to show that while traces could not prove the defendant "possessed" marijuana, they could be used to show that he "kept" marijuana in his apartment and that he was, therefore, "maintaining a nuisance."

Mr. Phelps wound up trying to distinguish between "keeping" and "possessing."

"Keeping is—keeping is very hard to say without using the word. Having on the premises, either in your custody or in the custody of someone else, a drug. In other words, Judge, this came out of the old liquor cases, like if someone came in and you have—he was invited into your place of business and you let him bring in his own bottle, that wouldn't be your own bottle, but he's keeping it on your premises and that would be against the law. That's what we're talking about here: keeping on the premises. If you have something on your premises—if you're keeping it there."

Judge Daly ruled for the time being that the "traces" could be used to support the contention that Steinbeck might have had knowledge that pot was smoked on his premises. However, the traces alone were not proof of anything; they would have to be connected with Steinbeck.

With the preliminaries more or less out of the way, Mr. Phelps called his first witness, Detective Edmond MacKinnon. Mr. MacKinnon, it developed, had over twelve years on the force and was in his sixth year on the narcotics squad. He had made hundreds of seizures of marijuana, possibly thirty in the year 1967.

He described the raid of October 16:

"When I arrived at the top-floor apartment I knocked on the door. The door was opened by a gentleman by the name of John Henry Fralich, whom I had met previously and I knew. I told Mr. Fralich that I had in my possession an arrest warrant for Jean Lasar and at the same time as I was talking to him I looked over his shoulder and I saw Miss Lasar sitting on a bunk bed . . . which would be to my right inside the apartment. I told Mr. Fralich that I had the warrant for Jean Lasar and I further went on to say, 'That's her sitting right there.' I walked in. I showed her the warrant, placed her under arrest. Right immediately in front, between her and myself, there was a form of a coffee table, a small table, which was cluttered with various items, but included laying on top of this coffee table was two smoking pipes. After I arrested Miss Lasar I advised her of her rights, and then reached down and picked up one of these two pipes and I smelled it, and from past experience I observed and could smell the odor of marijuana. After I observed the pipes and found that there had been marijuana in there and had been smoked, I further looked around the room and observed another girl who was later identified as a Nancy Marnett. I then placed the gentleman who let me in, Mr. Fralich, who I know to be a user of marijuana—I placed him under arrest and charged him with presence in an illegal establishment, to wit: a place where narcotics were found. After I placed Mr. Fralich under arrest he had on . . . a shirt and tie and pair of pants. There was a coat laying to one side which I could observe was the match to the pants Mr. Fralich had on. I asked him if it was his coat. He said it was and while handing him the coat, I, in the normal course of my duties, I felt through the pockets to make sure there was nothing in it and I removed a hard object from the inside coat pocket. It turned out to be a cigarette case which contained three cigarettes, freshly hand-rolled cigarettes of marijuana. I at that time then placed Mr. Fralich then under arrest and charged him with the marijuana tax act."

Having disposed of Fralich, the detective then took care of Jean Lasar.

"I diverted my attention back to Jean Lasar. She had on, as I recall—a shirt, a blue shirt, and she asked if I would hand her her pants. I think there was a pair of jeans. I gave her that. She put them on while still under the covers of the bed and at that time just to the foot of the bed, more or less, out to the center of the floor, was a Samsonite suitcase. I asked

Miss Lasar, I said, 'Whose suitcase is this?' She said, 'It is mine.' At that time I opened it and found it to contain four brown paper bags. Further examination revealed it to contain marijuana. I again asked Miss Lasar, 'This suitcase, do you know what's in it?' She says, 'Yes, there's about twenty pounds of marijuana in it.' "

Having found the four bags full, he had, in his professional phrase, "a new field exposed," so he searched the apartment and found a cigarette roller and "traces of marijuana" in a drawer which contained some of Steinbeck's clothes. This time the "traces" were thrown over rather abruptly.

"The traces are out," said the judge. "You ought to be ashamed to come in here with traces—I always said that—not for any reason."

Mr. Phelps asked for an opportunity "to organize an argument, because I know I am right and I haven't convinced you."

The judge declined.

"If you only have traces you can forget it. You can forget it," he said. "And I'm going to strike out all about that pipe too."

Mr. Phelps seemed alarmed. "Are you going to let me put the pipe in?"

"Unless," said the judge, "you show that this man had a pipe belonging to this man I'm going to strike it out . . ."

Phelps pleaded that the ownership of the pipe had nothing to do with the presence of marijuana. He said he was afraid he was "derailed."

"Well," said the judge, "don't argue with me; you've lost it. Don't they teach you when to stop. Now you're infuriating the court, so sit down."

"The last thing I want to do is that," Mr. Phelps said, referring of course to infuriating the court, not to sitting down, and he sat down.

Detective MacKinnon once more took over, and testified that he had also seized some typewritten papers that "had marijuana mentioned in them."

But the traces pretty much kicked over the first part of the prosecution. With them out, the case against Steinbeck seemed to have all but collapsed.

Everyone went to lunch.

When the court reconvened at two p.m. there had been some startling changes in the evidence. During the recess, the second government chemist, John Steele, the one who had examined the twenty pounds of weed from the suitcase and officially pronounced it marijuana, also examined the pipe and the tobacco pouch. He found enough marijuana in the pouch to make a cigarette and three times that amount in the pipe.

It was, it developed, the third time the pipe and pouch had been examined. The analyst Tannenbaum had first examined them and found nothing at all. Then at the insistence of Detective MacKinnon, he had reexamined it and had found the celebrated "traces."

Analyst Steele took the stand and said that he had received the pipe from Detective MacKinnon that lunch hour.

"I found this pipe containing a weedlike material. I took it back and I scraped out all the weedlike material. I found it contained one thousand and ten milligrams of a weedlike material before analysis and nine hundred and seventy milligrams of a weedlike material after analysis. On analysis and examination I found this material to be principally the leaf portion of the hemp plant *Cannabis sativa.*" He said he also found three hundred milligrams in the second tobacco pouch which had also been previously described as containing only "traces." Now remember, "traces" by definition are specks, hardly visible. The pouch, to focus on that for a moment rather than the pipe, was of a transparent kind. One would think that the first analyst, Mr. Tannenbaum, could have hardly failed to see a sizable chunk of marijuana weighing three hundred milligrams.

Mr. Lowe asked him to hold the pouch up for the jury to see, and said:

Q. Now, when you took yesterday at lunchtime the sub-

stance—keep holding it up—the substance out of the
pouch . . .

A. Yes?

Q. You didn't need a spatula to take that out, did you?

A. No.

Q. You just opened it up and it came out?

A. Yes.

And on continued cross-examination Mr. Steele said that
no competent chemist could conceivably find that the
amounts that fell out were only "traces." The same odd circumstances surrounded the pipe.

Detective MacKinnon was called back to the stand. He said
that after he first seized the pipe he put it loose in an envelope.
Later, at the narcotics-squad office, he put a strip of Scotch
Tape over the bowl. He was not sure how long a time elapsed
between the seizure and the sealing, possibly six or seven
hours, possibly eighteen or twenty. He then sent the pipe to
Tannenbaum, the chemist, in a sealed envelope. He said
he had not seen the pipe again until that very day when he
had gotten it back from Mr. Phelps. It appeared, he said, to
to be taped and sealed exactly as it had been when he first
sent it to be examined.

Judge Daly said that there was now no evidence that
chemist Tannenbaum had ever looked inside the bowl.

Defense attorney Lowe argued that "there has been no
showing how this—the one thousand milligrams—got into
the pipe, and I submit that's not sufficient evidence." He
added that had the loose lump of marijuana found by chemist
Steele been in the pipe originally, it would have fallen out
while it was being carried around by Detective MacKinnon
in a loose envelope.

MacKinnon replied that "the pipe top was crusted where
it had been previously smoked, which hardened there and as
a result there was nothing loose on the top." He admitted
that he had not seen any loose particle in the pipe.

Mr. Lowe once more pointed out that chemist Tannenbaum had examined the pipe after MacKinnon had sealed it and found only "traces."

Judge Daly asked the rather belated question, "Where is Tannenbaum?"

Mr. Phelps said he was on vacation, he didn't know where, and wouldn't be back until January. He suggested that the court disregard Tannenbaum's report as obviously erroneous.

"Naturally you're going to disregard it because it might be unfavorable to you," Judge Daly said. "Nevertheless the defense is entitled to have Mr. Tannenbaum explain . . . What do we know what he is going to say? You don't know what he's going to say."

The judge said he would entertain a motion from Mr. Lowe for a mistrial. Mr. Lowe said he didn't want a mistrial.

Mr. Lowe then called John Steinbeck IV to the stand, not only as the defendant, but also as an expert on marijuana.

Steinbeck first recounted the events of October 16 from his point of view:

"I woke up at about seven o'clock, which was the time I had to wake up. I had to be at duty at eight o'clock. There were some people staying in my apartment at the time and I got up, got dressed, and went to work. I had invited a John or Ian Fralich to stay with me. He was staying with me out of friendship, because he was being what I considered to be harassed by police. He couldn't stay with any friends, because the friends he did stay with were afraid that they too would then be subject to the same harassment, and not wanting such a thing to happen, I invited him to stay with me."

He said that the night before there had been some ten people in his apartment, most of whom he didn't know. They were the guests of Mr. Fralich.

When Steinbeck walked in on the group they were just sitting around, not smoking marijuana.

"I knew the jeopardy keeping Mr. Fralich at my apartment brought about and I asked him because of this, because I was in the United States Army, and subject to discipline under the Uniform Code of Military Justice, not to put me in a tight spot by having marijuana in the apartment. I didn't impose any other rules."

He added that he had not seen Fralich for some time before his arrival at the apartment on the 10th of October. He said he had seen Nancy and Jean on occasion, and that he knew Fralich smoked and that he suspected the girls did.

He said that when he woke up on the morning of October 16 he saw something alarming. "I saw in the kitchen four brown paper bags that were not there when I went to sleep the night before. At that point I suspected that they might contain marijuana. I didn't look in them, but I woke Ian Fralich up and I made it clear to him that if in fact those did contain marijuana I wanted them out of my apartment immediately. And then I went to work."

At work he told one of his superiors, a Major Walter H. Bowie, that he suspected that there was marijuana in his apartment and that he wanted him to know that it was none of his doing.

When he got home after work the raid had passed into history. The details of the great day and his subsequent arrest took, in fact, very little of witness Steinbeck's time. Most of the time he discoursed on marijuana, its use and abuse.

His having Ian Fralich as a house guest, it developed, was not pure hospitality.

"As a researcher in the sociological use of marijuana it is very valuable for me to speak with him, talk to him, live with him, and for those reasons he was staying with me."

People will often take positions in the artificial context of a courtroom that they would hesitate to take with a straight face in front of their friends. Mr. Steinbeck has, no doubt, an intellectual interest in marijuana, but being a "researcher in the sociological" seems to put a rather top-heavy twist to it.

He did make it clear that his interest in the weed was primarily that of a writer. He had, for example, written an account of his first interview with Detective MacKinnon and had offered it to the *Washingtonian*. It was the manuscript which Detective MacKinnon seized during the raid.

He had also written an article entitled "The Importance of Being Stoned in Vietnam," which was to appear in the January issue of the *Washingtonian*.

He testified that he had made an extensive study of pot in the East. . . .

"I covered just about every square mile of South Vietnam and was fortunate enough because of my job not to be stationed in any one place, but rather to report on the Vietnam scene for the United States Army."

He said he decided that approximately seventy-five per cent of the troops between nineteen and twenty-one smoked "the hemp plant *Cannabis sativa*."

"We have sociological groups of people, the United States soldiers who are absolutely not sure that they are going to be alive twenty-four hours later. As a result, there are next to no inhibitions in the Republic for smoking the plant. It is medically not a narcotic, that is to say you do not get an addiction for it as you do for even more commonplace vices, such as nicotine in cigarettes. This should be obvious to anyone who has ever tried to stop smoking."

Mr. Lowe asked Steinbeck his purpose in investigating marijuana. "I had become familiar with marijuana several years before I was drafted in the United States Army, and it's a subject of concern, I daresay, to everybody in this room. There are many parents whose children are in jail, or being prosecuted, or they are aware their children smoke it. There are many college professors who are aware their students smoke it. In this courthouse today I understand there are two other cases on the subject going on. This Christmas, I daresay, there are several hundred American youths under the age of twenty-five who are in jail or pending a prosecution on the use of the drug. For this reason it is not only a concern of mine, but probably of everybody who is intelligent or cares about the sociological use of such a thing."

On cross-examination prosecutor Phelps seemed inclined

to accept the notion that Steinbeck was a qualified expert on reefers.

Q. How is marijuana used?

A. *Cannabis sativa* can be used in many ways. It can be eaten, but in the quantities that American marijuana is grown it takes a great deal to get the effect desired, if you do indeed desire the effect. You can smoke it, and these are the two main ways that it is absorbed into the system.

Q. Have you ever seen anyone smoking marijuana?

A. Many times.

Q. Have you ever smoked marijuana?

A. I have experimented with it from time to time in my research.

Q. How frequently do you feel it necessary to experiment with it in your research?

A. To my satisfaction that I have experimented enough.

Q. Well how frequently is that, sir?

A. Infrequently.

Q. Once a week?

The court interrupted: "All right," Judge Daly said, "that's far enough. That has nothing to do with this charge."

The conversation then switched to the addictive qualities of marijuana.

Q. Sir, have you heard any reports in your research about marijuana coming from North Africa of such potency that people do get withdrawal [symptoms] with it?

A. As I understand it, it is a medical impossibility to undergo physical withdrawal from the active alkaloids of marijuana, which are two molecules of tetrahydracannabinol. Psychological addiction is possible to the same extent that a fat person is addicted to chocolate sundaes.

Q. Then, sir, you have not heard that marijuana of such a type as could cause withdrawal is being shipped into this country, is that correct?

A. I would question the source and I would also question the substance.

After further wandering around the hemp fields, Mr.

Phelps got to the more or less crucial question.

Q. Sir, you've testified that in your research occasionally or infrequently you have smoked marijuana. Have you smoked marijuana at seventeen thirty-seven F Street, or seventeen fifty-seven—I believe is the address?

A. Seventeen thirty-seven.

Q. Have you ever smoked marijuana there?

A. No.

After Steinbeck stepped down the defense called a character witness to testify, only, that Mr. Steinbeck had a very good reputation for truth and veracity among his friends.

The lawyers summed up their cases, Mr. Phelps making it a point that Mr. Steinbeck's distinguished heritage was of no consequence since "we do not have earls and we do not have dukes in this country."

The judge instructed the jury. In English courts they often say that a judge sums up either for or against a defendant. British judges have, as a matter of fact, a good deal more freedom in comment than do Americans. An American judge is in charge, as it were, of the law. The judge can tell them, in the limitations of the law, how the facts are to be applied.

The case against Steinbeck was that he "maintained a nuisance" by permitting narcotic users to congregate in his home.

The evidence against him consisted clearly of the fact that a couple of people with pot on their persons or, more exactly, in their possession, had been arrested there.

Less clear was the confused evidence about the marijuana in the pipe.

The last element in the case was the subtle one of continuity. The maintenance of a nuisance is not, by common-law definition, a single isolated thing. The nuisance must be shown to have had a past as well as a present, though how long a past is very vague indeed.

On the business of the "traces" the judge said: "There is in evidence ... a report ... from a chemist to whom this material was originally given, and those reports, which you may take to the jury room with you, show that the chemist found only traces and nothing more on the pipe and in the tobacco pouch . . . Originally, one report shows that originally he found nothing and then on a second examination he found traces. Now you do have additional testimony of another examination of the pipe and the tobacco pouch by Mr. Steele and he testified what he found, which you heard. But in the event that you are not satisfied with the testimony of Mr. Steele and you feel that maybe only traces were evidenced by this pipe and this tobacco pouch, and it contained nothing more than traces, then you are instructed that as a matter of law . . . traces are insufficient evidence to prove the guilt of a person keeping illegal narcotics. Traces of themselves, which is not a usable amount, are insufficient to convict this man of the crime with which he is charged."

On the question of the continuity of the nuisance—if a nuisance there was—the judge said: " . . . if you find that nuisance actually existed you must find that the marijuana which is alleged to have been kept on the premises was actually a pattern of conduct of a recurring and continuous nature . . . the law does not specifically define the duration or length of time that this wrongdoing must exist. The law doesn't say it has to exist for five minutes, or it has to exist for one month, or it has to exist for one week, but it does require proof beyond a reasonable doubt that this course of conduct actually commenced and that it had existed for a time prior to the search of these premises on October 16. That's what the government must prove beyond a reasonable doubt."

The jury heard the judge and went out for some forty-five minutes and returned to find John Steinbeck IV not guilty. A jury member told him to "keep up the good work." One might wonder what good work he had in mind. One could guess that it had something to do with a self-conscious young man trying to explain something, and a middle-aged jury and a middle-aged judge trying to understand. Prosecutor Phelps, incidentally, and perhaps irrelevantly, is in his twenties; defense attorney Lowe is in the first cool blush of middle age.

V I

When I first read Kelly's article I couldn't quite identify myself or the police, or the prosecutor, with the sincerity and focus that he gave us. I know I was hoping to get a not-guilty verdict and I didn't feel it was useful to give the jury any more than they needed to arrive at that verdict. During those days I was being harassed by the Department of Motor Vehicles, who were trying to take away my driver's license just because my name had been tied in with marijuana. This struck me as peculiar and unusual, not to mention unfair. And I was being confronted in court with what looked like an attempt to plant marijuana in my pipe midway in the trial, an attempt engineered by officials I would have preferred to believe would not stoop to that level. More than ever I felt that the establishment was out to enforce the law, or whatever interpretation they extracted from the law, for the sake of enforcement rather than for morality or public health.

I was still dealing with the Department of Motor Vehicles a month later. They took the stand that they could and would revoke my license until such time as I could prove that I was medically fit to drive an automobile. Apparently they had used this threat, and made it stick, with many young people involved with marijuana offenses. I returned with my own challenge that they had better prove I was unfit before I would turn in my license. I ended up in the office of a doddering public-health official who, while taking a sample of my urine, couldn't stop talking about marijuana use when he was a college boy. I talked to him about the test and although he didn't admit it in so many words he indicated that he agreed with me that the test was stupid and could not really prove anything about my use of marijuana. This was the official who would sign the paper that would satisfy the Department of Motor Vehicles. I am certainly no medical expert, but I had studied the subject sufficiently to know that there is no medical test which could show that because of marijuana I wasn't fit to drive a car. It seemed impossible to me that public-health officials at any level really believed in this test. Could they be kidding themselves or someone else? To prove something or other to myself or anyone else who might be interested I smoked marijuana and hashish right before taking the urine test and just as I thought, no sign of it could be detected. Urine tests do reveal heroin, and this was just one more instance of marijuana being linked inaccurately with heroin. I was duly restored to the status of responsible driver and heard no more from the Department of Motor Vehicles.

After the trial I was invited to a number of Washington society parties, around New Year's Eve, and at every one I went to there were people who wanted to know about marijuana. Around eleven o'clock, or the time when alcohol had loosened all inhibitions, these solid citizens were asking me if I could get them any marijuana. These were the people who really are the support and foundation for the laws which had almost put me in jail, and yet they could barely wait to ask me to get some for them. I know my experience was not special to me because I have enough friends who are admitted marijuana users who have had the same requests from other upright taxpayers.

My marijuana experience might have ended with the trial, but with the publication of the *Washingtonian* piece a few days before the trial I suddenly fell into the position of being considered a spokesman for any subject, and people were ready to assume that I would have something meaningful to say about abortion, civil rights, North Vietnam, black power, as well as marijuana and the hippies. More out of curiosity than anything else, I cooperated and appeared on various TV programs. Apparently there was a need and a readiness for the morning audiences to hear about marijuana from an admitted user. I wasn't as exotic as Allen Ginsberg, but that was maybe even better. People didn't really want to be offended by what they heard and I had acquired the dubious reputation of being inoffensive. Ginsberg, like Tim Leary, had developed a wonderful habit of infuriating and confusing the older generation, but here I was, a Vietnam veteran, with a little beard, yes, but I had short hair. Mothers would like to hear me talk about American youth.

One day I received a phone call from the Senate Subcommittee on Juvenile Delinquency. A staff member named Mr. Mooney said that my article on drugs in Vietnam had come to their attention and would I have lunch with him and discuss the details of the article more fully. I said yes, and so we did. Of all the people who had asked me questions about marijuana in Vietnam, Mr. Mooney seemed to be the most informed. He had talked with Vietnam veterans about drugs, including amphetamines, over a year before in a Senate action to try and get the military to come across with believable figures. Mr. Mooney told me that the subcommittee had known about the drug use in Vietnam for quite a while but they had never been able to get the witnesses to testify about anything more than a few isolated incidents. About a year earlier they had a sergeant who was a helicopter gunner and he testified about killing some friendly forces when he was a little too excited on a mission one day with the help of too many pills. He wasn't smoking marijuana but rather taking barbiturates. He had told the subcommittee that a great many drugs were being used in

Vietnam. The subcommittee had kept on trying to get the Army to tell them what was really going on, but it seemed impossible to get a witness who had enough information to force the Army to really accept the challenge. Up until this time the only reaction that I had had from what I considered to be the government side of the marijuana question was one of complete disbelief. The subcommittee left me with the impression that they knew everything I had said was true; they just wanted me to say it in public again. They asked that I testify in front of Senate hearings with Dr. Goddard, then the director of the Bureau of Food and Drug Administration, at some date in the near future.

In his State of the Union Message, President Johnson had asked Congress to give him funds to add hundreds of new federal narcotics officials to the ranks. This message was delivered at about the same time as my first talks with Mr. Mooney. Johnson had made a particular point about LSD. The day after the speech LSD was very much in the news but with the added fillip that a Pennsylvania Commissioner for the Blind had perpetrated a hoax by inventing a story about three college students who had gone blind while using LSD and staring at the sun. The commissioner was inspired by some of that strange zeal which I had seen at work in the marijuana search-and-destroy tactics used by narcotics agents on the trail of marijuana. There was some speculation that Johnson had only mentioned LSD because of this twisted commissioner's earlier inflammatory reports about the imaginary incident. If this was so, the President's speechwriters did our leader a disservice. At any rate, Johnson wanted the penalties for drug use increased, but he had a problem. Goddard had already come out saying that he thought the existing penalties for the use of LSD and marijuana were too severe. The hearing date set for the Senate subcommittee was postponed and postponed because Johnson seemed to be blocking any testimony by Goddard which didn't agree with his feelings about the drugs. It seemed curious to me that Johnson would follow the advice of his expert generals on the war strategy but he thought that the country's experts on drugs weren't intelligent enough to advise him about drug laws.

A date for the hearings was finally set in February and they opened with testimony from Goddard. Senator Dodd, the esteemed chairman, first asked Goddard if he had his presidential muzzle on. Goddard replied that he had never been muzzled by President Johnson. He went on to say that he did not think that the use of marijuana should carry such stiff penalties and he added that penal advisers whose field of expertise was punishment rather than pharmacology had convinced him that present penalties were the only course to be taken to stem the abuse of marijuana. There was a patent contradiction in this point of view and Goddard had to endure a lot of cross-questioning about it. How could it be that Goddard personally thought the penalties too much and the penologists thought they were just right? Goddard stuck to his two guns throughout and managed only to confuse the issue by insisting on his right to his personal views but his loyal support of the penal experts to carry on as usual if not more so. To me it seemed like more and more of the contradiction that existed everywhere I turned whether it was voiced by well-intentioned parents or high government officials. I won't say it was hypocritical; it is more subtle than that. But I thought more than ever that the smog needed to be cleared away from the marijuana issue somehow.

In his testimony Goddard went on to describe the many control measures which had been taken by his department. Then he was faced with the embarrassing task of telling the Senate subcommittee that despite all of this, the use of marijuana was still sharply on the increase. In fact, there seemed to be a direct ratio in operation: the more controls that were enforced against marijuana, the more marijuana abuse there was.

As the hearings proceeded all the federal officials who had been called to testify came armed with extensive dossiers telling the grim story of how terrible marijuana was. These officials related countless grisly tales of armed robbery, rape, and murder, all committed by people with "marijuana histories." One official, in response to a question about the use of marijuana by nice college kids, said that he attributed the growing increase of marijuana abuse on campuses to be directly related to the rise in intelligence level of the users, who with their increased *articulation* had a way of promoting the drug faster than government agencies could stamp it out. Officials were having to watch out for those fast-talking collegians. At this point it was not clear whether or not the question had turned from the use of drugs to the abuse of intelligence.

I was impressed with the Senate subcommittee staff. At this level there seemed to be far less prejudice than I had expected on the subject of marijuana. For the most part they seemed to be a group of people who really wanted to find out what was going on. They were very aware that the more violent critics of marijuana were probably suffering from a puritanical streak that had no place in today's scientific sophistication. At one time I would have thought that the people on such a staff would be precisely the people I would have to fight, but they too wanted to know and consider what was with marijuana. The problem was that their advisers didn't know anything.

There was a unique woman who did testify at the hearings in an extraordinarily intelligent manner. This was Helen H. Nowlis, Ph.D. She is the director of the Drug Education Project of the National Association of Student Personnel Administrators. She is a professor of psychology and research consultant to the Office of the Provost, University of Rochester. Despite her credentials, she seemed bothered, as well she might be, by the bright lights and the other confusions and distractions which attend Senate hearings.

Helen Nowlis opened by challenging the idea of "drug use" as compared to "drug abuse." The narcotics officials can make no such distinctions, of course. Use is abuse, possession is abuse, being present where drugs exist is abuse, in terms of the laws they enforce. This patent absurdity makes intelligent discussion difficult. Searching for some clarification, Dr. Nowlis compared studies indicating that about seventy per cent of the U.S. population has used alcohol (our most popular drug), if use is defined as ever having tried it. Millions of Americans fall into each of the following categories: no present use, occasional use, regular use, heavy use, problem use, and plain alcoholism. In responding to questions about drug abuse among students she was at an instant impasse. Dr. Nowlis was quick to point out that no reliable studies exist regarding student use or abuse of drugs since any statistical study is suspect due to misunderstanding and misinterpretation of the words "use" and "abuse." She volunteered that her acquaintance with available studies, and her wide knowledge acquired dealing directly with students, suggested there was no national emergency. She said that the "life-shattering penalties" inhibit any serious investigation into the area of drug use, and she stressed the fact that use of marijuana and LSD is not confined to ornery and rebellious adolescents.

Dr. Nowlis thought the problem closely related to the "pressures and discontents of our society especially at the professional and executive level, plus the fact the American people have apparently bought the well-advertised proposition that there is a chemical cure for any malaise . . . coupled with a complete misunderstanding of what drugs are and how they act." The result is a new disease, elegantly known as "status medicamentosis"—more casually known in the medical profession (often seen by hospital-admissions people) as "the brown-paper-bag syndrome." This refers to patients with a wide variety of symptoms who when asked to bring all medications they are using appear with so many they require a sizable sack. Nowlis remarked that the drug industry has replaced the automobile industry as the number-one profit-making industry in the country. We want our cars and our drugs and we have a plenitude of both. Nowlis "wished that every one of you [the subcommittee] had to face

thoughtful young people who may or may not use marijuana
. . . who ask why a bill regulating mail-order sale of guns,
which do kill and maim more people, both accidentally and
intentionally, than all drugs put together, cannot get to first
base . . . or explain why alcohol, which ruins the lives of
countless millions and has been demonstrated to be widely
associated with crimes of violence [not to mention over sixty-
five per cent of traffic fatalities, she might have added], is
extensively advertised and promoted and freely available to
all adults."

The subcommittee members listened politely but they
seemed unmoved by such ringing declarations as this: "These
are not stupid, abnormally rebellious young people . . . they
are intelligent students at a stage in their lives in which one
of their main tasks is to search for values which will serve
them in their own time and in their own place!" Anyone
for values? I doubted it then; I still doubt it; but I am hopeful another generation will come along with that word, and
all it means, as part of their everyday vocabulary.

Many men on the subcommittee (and all the reporters) had
heard this kind of statement before. Dr. Nowlis's impas-
sioned delivery should have given the ideas new zest, but
nearly everyone present appeared bored, waiting for her to
finish. She emphasized that "no Pied Piper comes offering
these wares" (the whole list of things, legal and illegal, which
high-school students are exploring, including marijuana,
LSD, Green Dragon, Hawaiian wood-rose, morning-glory
seeds, mescaline, cough syrup, nutmeg, cloves, etc.). "Part of
the game is seeking and finding. It might behoove us to look
for the reasons why . . . so much of their time and energy is
spent on finding and taking these substances . . . but that takes
much more time to do . . . than to bring out the big stick."
She was convinced that more agents (undercover or overt)
will certainly put more students in jail but will not eliminate
marijuana use. She spoke pertinently to the question of the
law: "We [teachers] are dedicated to teaching, by example as

well as precept, respect for the law of the land, and if the law is not a just law, to work to change it."

I found myself agreeing completely with Dr. Nowlis and I wondered if there were others in the room who also agreed. It was impossible to tell; dutiful courtesy was the prevailing mood. In talking with members of the subcommittee staff later I felt they were exceptionally perceptive—however they bring about no legislation.

Dr. Nowlis ended her testimony by urging that all criminal sanctions for possession of marijuana be removed; she thought there was no need for it to be legalized at this time. This is obviously the right direction to proceed. I would concur completely with her that drug abuse of any kind, in fact *abuse* of any kind, is a serious problem to be dealt with basically by means of health education, while the matter of "values" is kept in the foreground of all serious efforts to deal with abuse in any area. We plainly are now a drug culture, accepting and depending on "the false belief that life can and should be freed of all pain, tension, irritation, unhappiness through the use both of drugs and of chemical substances we prefer not to call drugs—this worries me far more than the current use of marijuana by college students." Exit Dr. Nowlis and enter some agents with inflammatory tales of the latest raids and arrests by the ever-vigilant narcotics squad. The subcommittee could not help but seem more interested in the excitement that accompanies sleuthing and tracking down whatever quarry.

I found myself adding to Dr. Nowlis's list of things people expect to be freed of—odor? appetite? reality? There are an awful lot of deodorants sold, a lot of hunger suppressants, a lot of cosmetics for both living and dead, a lot of entertainment, a lot of insurance and protection for every possible minor inconvenience and major disaster. The hustlers offer values to us constantly at very reduced prices. I think if Gallup polled a sample of the American middle class and asked, "What is a value?" this would be met by, "The value of

F

what?" If the pollster persisted with, "What is the value of anything to you?" the answer probably would be given in dollars and cents because the word has no other coinage.

When my turn to testify came, Senator Dodd introduced me very handsomely. I felt odd being introduced so flatteringly by a man with such a questionable reputation. He said that although the subcommittee had heard from many experts, including enforcement officials, academic researchers, and members of the medical profession, it was in the interest of learning more about the marijuana situation to hear from a member of a younger generation who had investigated this field and who had opinions which might be valuable to these proceedings. I was given the same courteous attention which the older generation was afforded.

Prior to this I had submitted (according to instructions) a ten-page statement where I tried to answer a long list of questions posed by Senator Dodd. Thus, I gathered that he, and the other subcommittee members, had read this statement in advance of my appearance. Nevertheless I was asked to read my statement aloud, which I did. (See Appendix II for this statement.) I was made to feel that there was no hurry and I could take all the time I might want to recount my views and amplify, if I chose, the prepared statement. There were frequent interruptions, questions from Dodd or other subcommittee members about some point in passing. Whereas they had often seemed politely bored with Dr. Nowlis's approach to the situation, they often seemed politely pained by my replies.

After I had finished my part I sat there listening to the many others who had been invited to appear, cherishing a naïve hope that perhaps this kind of occasion was really the heart of government. I had often visited Congress when it was in session and I had been appalled at how few Congressmen were ever present. Someone had explained that the real work of legislation was accomplished in the committee and subcommittee meetings; the absent Congressmen were ostensibly off at such meetings, coming to grips with the nation's problems. I realized it was unlikely, if not impossible, that the chairman would wind up the session with some kind of summarizing statement. But I had hoped to sense some quickening of mood on the part of the subcommittee members, some sign that they could and would act as a more informed body now that they had received such a quantity of information. This was far from the case. The attendance of the subcommittee members began to drop off before the hearings were complete; it was evident that interest was definitely slackening. Cynically, I tried to calculate what this event may have cost the taxpayers. Each of us who testified was paid a nominal stipend. It did not add up to any great total; probably the taxpayers would not resent footing this bill or similar bills from the umpteen other subcommittee hearings that take place.

At *what* invisible price? To *what* self-defeating end? What would be the value? Dr. Nowlis had raised these questions in regard to the proposed increase of narcotics agents who would, of course, be able to increase student arrests. The question stood, rhetorically, unanswered. When Frank Giordano of the Bureau of Drug Abuse Control testified for the official establishment, supporting the idea of a massive increase in narcotics agents, there was no apparent paradox. When physicians testified, pointing out that marijuana was not addictive or harmful, this was duly noted, no more. It was not a debate in a vacuum; there was no debate. It was unnecessary, irrelevant, and impossible for Senator Dodd (of all people) to offer any real summing-up of the total testimony. All of us were enfolded in the classically liberal embrace and we could feel comfortably relieved this kind of wonderful forum, right next to the heart of government, was possible, was happening—and we were part of it!

When Senator Dodd was bringing the hearings to a close, all benevolent kindness and courtesy, I had a strong impulse to leap to my feet and put one more question: "What value has our combined testimony been to you?" and then declare a one-man sit-in until some satisfactory reply was proffered. Of course I didn't and the session ended on a very polite note whereby we could all smile at each other, unity in diversity, Americans all. We could and would now return to our specialties. The newsmen would blow up my so-called controversial remarks about marijuana in Vietnam; they would largely ignore the more important pleas of Dr. Nowlis. The physicians who had offered their expertise to the effect that marijuana was not harmful or addictive were now free to return to their special world. The Senators would hurry to their busy rounds of politicking in an election year. Democracy was working as usual, each of us "doing our thing" in a kind of horrible, fragmenting, canceling-out process where the sum of all our parts ended up with much less significance than any single individual might offer.

To escape such thoughts one might get high, or drunk, or philosophical. For the moment I tried the last as I searched around in my mind to pick up reassuring glimmers from my magpie reading which would tell me all was not as bad as it seemed. I promised myself that the much-heralded General Systems Theory was being hammered out in some genius's brain, somewhere in the world, far from the heart of any government, and there would be a quantum leap someday into a unity bred of diversity bringing about a wholeness between human beings. The subcommittee hearings did not and could not have any fixed value; maybe they were a part of the whole groping toward something else. Each of us who took part was a particular product of the input-output educational system, no one of us necessarily better than any other, each operating according to some code or system we had learned to believe in. Dodd had made his personal dilemma abundantly clear to the world not long before; he had lived by the unwritten Senate code, much to the embarrassment of the other Senators when he was caught. Giordano was simply fulfilling his part as a truly professional "catcher," a product of the best law-enforcement training the U.S. can offer. Psychologist Nowlis exemplified the open-system approach in fruitless impasse with the closed-systems. The reporters were wide open in receiving material, but to get out "the story" they had to funnel everything through a very limited system. Overreaching all of us was a vague socio-ethical system made up of a mixture of all the codes men ever developed and have been reluctant to really review or synthesize: the Hippocratic Oath (pertinent about 500 B.C.) and the Ten Commandments (given not much more than lip service but still hanging in there), and the Magna Carta, the Bill of Rights, common-sense flat-earthers along with Copernican and Newtonian physics, Darwinian evolutionary theory, Einsteinian relativity, even suffrage—all of it smudged together according to the second law of thermodynamics so that we can still smile politely, homeostatically, at each other no matter how we differ. We can meet in the "cool" forum (or was it a latter-day Roman circus for us to let off steam?) and believe that we are quite advanced for we are at least exchanging ideas whether or not anything is merged or forged.

Meanwhile one must take comfort in the fact that there are a few innovators and synthesizers in the fields of sociology, biology, chemistry, and philosophy busily exploring within and without their specialties, all motivated by an equal ultimate concern for humanity. Maybe the "cool" circus, where anyone can testify, is an ideal interim. As biologist Lorenz has said, "Perhaps the long sought missing-link between animals and the really humane being is ourselves!" Thus, our paradoxes, our strange circuses, within and without government, are simply inexorable steps in our evolution toward a greater good at some future date.

THREE

AT EASE

Not long after the Senate hearings, I drove to California with my old school friend Al. We planned to stop all along the way west to visit with friends and see some of the more spectacular parts of the country. The itinerary was vague but we promised ourselves wide margins and sparkling checkpoints which would illumine the trip.

I had to bring Al up to date on all the Washington activities and that meant resaying and rethinking the whole marijuana situation. I was becoming so terribly bored with the subject I could barely discuss it. Al chided me for taking this attitude—whether I had planned it or not, I had become a minor celebrity just because of marijuana. On his campus, Yale, my name was connected with marijuana irrevocably and the impression existed that I was stamping around on a white charger, taking the rap for all marijuana users, going full tilt at the establishment, and, they hoped, trying to bring down all the legal prohibitions. Just in order that marijuana could settle quietly, uneventfully, into the landscape and be of no more special interest than shoes and ships and sealing-wax, I told him I only wished I could feel my role in the marijuana situation had accomplished something. Central to my *malaise* was the depressing feeling I had fallen into the same trap as the narcotics officials by joining them in making simple marijuana larger than life by having such a loud opinion one way or the other about it. One of the famous Zen anecdotes came to mind: the distraught Zen student comes to his teacher but the monk asks him: "Why do you seek solutions when there is no problem?" As many people—lawyers, doctors, professors, as well as myself—have agreed, the problem about marijuana is the unreal laws, not the drug itself.

Perhaps it is too early to evaluate the results of the Senate hearings, and the umpteen other medical and legal findings which are accumulating in a steady stream, all of them emphasizing marijuana is not dangerous and the present laws should be changed to fit truth and reality. But because it was marijuana which launched my name into the news media and because I have only the friendliest regard for the drug, I decided then I owed myself, and perhaps some readers, a factual account of these recent months, in order to make my part in the proceedings clearer to me, and to those readers. With such an account completed I hoped to feel free to let my mind explore several other areas which are of much greater interest and significance to me.

The ride itself acted to flush our minds clean, with new unmemorized places flashing by. Every stop became a curiously significant pause in pace as each new surrounding glowed in our awareness of it, becoming a special place to be, a place where we could literally exist in a way one does not when camping in some rented city apartment. We quoted the realtor's phrase "If you lived here, you'd be home right now" to each other on mountaintops, down in caverns, deep in forests, out on the desert. Our new, fast Detroit luxury road-mobile that was the freight, as well as the freighter, turned into a location module, hurrying our senses from place to place with such grace the going itself became a frictionless bubble of childish delight. The act of passing through so much and so varied an environment seemed to filter off sedimentary preoccupations. Although compatible, stimulating, or necessary stops along the way made up the mechanics for getting from here to there, it was the moving exposure of the mind itself that wove the spell of the journey.

We were reminded of Alan Watts's metaphor for this sensation: to the listener, the point of the music is not to reach the end. The reason for the living statement of music is that it unfolds itself, note by note. It is not to be known as a whole, or as having any goal or specific point other than the actual "changing" of it from phrase to phrase with an aimless determination that makes savoring it seem like it is for the first time, every time. Western listeners may feel this with symphonic music, but more strikingly with baroque, which is akin to the endlessly unfolding patterns of the Indian sitar repertoire. As we tore out of the cold East, the industrial scenery flew past while the images in the movie theater of our minds remained as effortlessly close as the moon skipping along over the trees.

We camped out one night on a razorback mountain in the Ozarks. The moonlight was so bright we decided to fly some kites an editor had given me in New York. These were very delicate Indian fighting kites, made of colored tissue paper and bamboo, extremely light and responsive. There was the softest of misty breezes, yet they soared like birds right out of our hands into the air. We had thousands of feet of mono- filament line and very rapidly they swept off into the sky, dancing, pivoting, swooping like gay little bats. All the better to see them and to salute the occasion, we set off a bar- rage of fireworks we'd purchased earlier in the evening.

We had passed through a town where they were sold, so we took advantage of the opportunity to fulfill an old child- hood power-wish to pick out and set off all the fireworks we liked. We used the geographical idiosyncrasies of the con- tinental United States, that night, and others, as the backdrop and sounding box for our dazzling combinations of whistling rockets, smart reports, and aesthetic explosions. We stopped many times, at other mountain crests, to stand side by side to do battle with our kites or to commune with what we agreed could be a muse of pyrotechnical poetry. Even if we lit only one giant skyrocket at a time, the person who lit the fuse took artistic responsibility for the success or failure of the event. We became convinced that the Japanese fireworks manufacturers are sensitive to this natural tendency for the fuse lighter to feel like a creator, because all these identical bombs are extraordinarily different in character. Some don't work and some work too well. The silent activity of the duds milk suspense from already jangled nerves with a mocking, lingering fizzle of sparks. Even with these draining pitfalls, the narcotic in them all works well enough to leave the match holder with the illusive impression that no matter what happens the project is remarkable and worth the delicate joke of truly being the fool waiting on the edge of his seat for the event to happen, even if what indeed happens is the absence of any event.

The Ozarks were a long way from Saigon, but the multicolored showers of sparks, the zooming flares, the paper parachutes which popped out of the sizzling whistles, reminded me of those evenings when with other Saigon Warriors we would sip gin or smoke marijuana, and watch the war from the rooftop bars of all the hotels in the city. The experience had always made me think of a description I read about aristocratic English officers watching their regiments wheel and turn on the battlefield which lay in front of them like an immense billiard table. During the preparations for a larger battle, the officers had social outings, picnics, where they set up buffets of delicacies on nearby high ground in order to witness better the finer aspects of preliminary skirmishes before the big event—I think it was Waterloo—which was to be scheduled in that area at some later time.

In Saigon, the Viet Cong were constantly infiltrating the suburbs and the nearby air bases: they would suddenly launch a close-in mortar attack, or run through a supply compound, blowing up ammunition pads with satchel charges. The Americans would reply by launching a rapid series of air strikes on the edge of town, coupled with a shower of flares which would hang in the air like floating diadems. Key areas would be circled with helicopter gunships, careening around like giant dragonflies. Another hors d'oeuvre for this evening cocktail entertainment would be served as one more exploding ammunition pad would erupt into a brilliant holocaust, lighting the sky completely and, at first, soundlessly, with white, then yellow. Immediately our senses would be pounded by the familiar blast of air which preceded the shattering *crack-k-k!!!* Then the colors would mingle into a searing orange. This sort of thing happened every night. I recall one night when I sat with a delicate Vietnamese bar girl and as I stared out at the spectacle she grabbed my arm, clinked my glass with hers, and inquired, "Beaucoup chin-chin, Ho Chi Minh?" I can't say I was above it all because quiet nights in Saigon were mostly remarkable when, like fireworks, their lack of interest made you want to dive back into the box for another one.

As we drove west the radio kept us in touch with other parts of the world. We were advised that in Boston, that day, twenty-nine students at a big medical school had formed a committee and appeared before the dean, to demand certain reforms in the curriculum. Also, twenty-nine students at the same school had been arrested in a marijuana raid. Probably not the same students, we thought, but then again it just might be.

Al's brother is in medical school, and we talked about the new look which today's medical students are insisting upon. Gone is the emphasis on crisis medicine, despite the news media's hysteria about heart transplants. Our generation's doctors (and many of their teachers) are ready for an approach which anticipates and prevents sickness rather than being almost totally concerned with administering and managing disease as an older generation's physicians have been. Maybe crisis medicine ("Nurse . . . forceps, please") is war; health is peace.

I tried to explain to Al why I wanted to return to Vietnam if I had really found the war so depressing. My main reason in returning would be to experience some of the peacetime qualities of the people there. Although the United States has had pacification programs (far beyond and exceeding any similar efforts ever made in history) in Vietnam for years, and although the people have adapted amazingly to the incessant war, there is much about the country I want to become familiar with as a civilian. Just as the GI's stationed in Europe see it differently when they return out of uniform, I, along with many other young Americans, have an urge to return to the place where we lived through one of the most impressionable times of our lives. I think Asia will become for my contemporaries what Europe became for older Americans. The confrontation with the Japanese in World War II did not stir up this same appreciation of Asia because, except for a favored few who lived for a while in Japan, most Americans knew the Japanese only as "slant-eyed devils," "kamikaze maniacs," etc.

Al reminded me I might run into flocks of doves in Vietnam after President Johnson's dramatic announcements in February 1968 promising some really peaceful overtures at last. If the attitudes on Vietnam (and marijuana) were to change or shift even a little in my direction I might be in the ironic position of crying out so loudly against the more obvious injustices of the world that I failed to hear the reports which showed things were going my way in spite of myself. Vietnam, as I had known it, would be quite altered, I was sure, whether or not peace was in the air. I've moved around the world enough to know it is the movement of the living which made the memories in the first place. If the tempo changed, my memories of Vietnam, already old and familiar as photographs, would be put away. What Asia would say to me and do to me when I returned would be something I couldn't know until I'd lived through it.

We stopped at Fort Sill to see another school friend who is there in the Army, soon to be shipped to Vietnam. He, too, was anxious to ask me about all the marijuana publicity. I promised him an autographed copy of the book I would

write about it. Relieved to talk about something else, we
enjoyed mystifying Al with our military gossip. The general
richness of the federal language makes you sound like a paranoid adult talking about sex in front of children. All the
terms were still fresh in my mind, and we had a lot of fun
trying to see how complex a conversation we could have using
Army acronyms: What's the SOP for your AIT in NCO
school? Will that change your MOS so that your TDY will
become OJT? until your ETS? Maybe, he replied, and that's
OK, if I don't get PCS to the NAM and get KIA'd.* We three
had been having reunions so regularly that for all intents and
purposes we had never been really separated. Now it looked
like the practice might continue overseas.

We happened on a radio symposium where selected
parents, physicians, lawyers, were discussing marijuana. A
doctor was quoted as saying *Cannabis* does not have the
"criminogenic action so unquestionably accepted by the
police and press." Someone read from a piece of anti-mari-
juana literature titled *The Assassin of Youth* which held that
"Every marijuana cigarette is loaded with immorality, de-
basing perversions, hatred, brutality, sex crimes, sadistic
murder, insanity and suicide." I was driving then and asked
Al to write it down for me; I knew I could never pass up a
chance to quote *that* line. A motherly-sounding lady quoted
a California State PTA study of marijuana which sounded
exactly like the Nowlis testimony before the Senate. The
study concluded by saying today's emphasis on law enforcement and punitive measures "has not been successful in controlling or reducing marijuana." Hooray for the PTA! It
was the mixture, as before, and other news items jumped off
the radio reporting the never-ending arrests for marijuana
offenses.

* SOP stands for Standard Operating Procedure; AIT for Advanced Indi-
vidual Training; NCO for Non-Commissioned Officer; MOS for Military
Occupational Specialty; TDY for Temporary Duty; OJT for On the Job
Training; ETS for Estimated Termination of Service; PCS for Permanent
Change of Station; NAM for Vietnam; KIA for Killed in Action.

A prominent California politician, Jesse Unruh, delivered a blast, saying Hubert Humphrey's entry into the presidential race would only splinter the hope for unity; Unruh was Robert Kennedy's man in California and there is no doubt Hubert was unwanted in that camp. Almost without a pause we heard a report about Unruh's nineteen-year-old son who was involved in a two-count felony marijuana offense. We agreed we would probably like the son more than the father, and we speculated about how the change in official attitudes (PTA's, doctors, lawyers, professors are not to be confused with "officials," although I'm not sure what a real "official" is) would come, paradoxically, from the users themselves. This would bear out the Yin and the Yang of it. When the radio informed us Kingman Brewster (president of Yale) was now experiencing how it is to have his son picked up in a raid over spring vacation at Martha's Vineyard—we felt the next flash would have to involve Lynda Bird. Maybe that would do it and the whole silly business would then be seen to be a bubble that would pop and everyone would know there was only a void, nothing to be terrified of at all. We were working on this bubble metaphor, tying it to a Taoist idea that all usefulness comes from voids, that only empty hands can hold something—and it was time to buy gas.

At the gas station there were some immense "Bubble-matic Guns" with which you could fire out showers of iridescent bubbles. We bought one on the spot and later, when we camped on the rim of the Grand Canyon, we were enraptured with blowing bubbles. We had a regular bubble blower, too, and we discovered we could inhale a big drag of cigarette smoke, then blow a bubble, which would contain the smoke; when the bubble hit the ground and broke, the smoke fluffed out and drifted off. We felt we were seeing Zen realized by something or other almost hourly; Oriental philosophy illustrations were as ubiquitous as Volkswagens. We would start talking about something in serious, level tones, but by the time we had exchanged a few semiprofundities and mocked each other, we would end up with improvised Zen riddles, laughing like a couple of jolly monks.

Al and I are both seriously interested in meditation. He told me how the Student International Meditation Society was growing like wildfire at all the campuses. In prep school we had sporadically performed a few of the Hatha Yoga exercises, sitting in the lotus position, feeling very high on self-induced spirituality. We had "discovered" the much-quoted Tao Te Ching by Lao-tzu at the same time one snowy winter day, and we had both memorized it then in the flush of adolescence. We recited it aloud again with renewed, pragmatic understanding, Al taking one line, me the next, joining in a loud crescendo in the final statement, half reciting, half singing:

> The secret waits for the insight
> of eyes unclouded by longing;
> those who are bound by desire
> see only the outward container.
>
> Thirty spokes will converge
> in the hub of a wheel;
> but the use of the cart
> will depend on the part
> of the hub that is void.
>
> With a wall all around
> a clay bowl is molded;
> but the use of the bowl
> will depend on the part
> of the bowl that is void.
>
> So advantage is had
> from whatever is there;
> but usefulness rises
> from whatever is not.

The new thing that is exciting the young people was largely inspired by Maharishi Mahesh Yogi. He was popularizing a particular technique which is foolproof for the simple reason that we are the perfectly finite creatures we are. You don't have to believe it; just meditate, as per instructions, and it works. Al's descriptions reminded me of my mother telling me it didn't matter whether I liked carrots or not, when I was a little boy; just go ahead and eat them anyway—*good* for you. And when I wanted to be able to play the trumpet beautifully and I balked at practicing, I was urged to keep the faith and just practice every day and I would amaze myself; I was promised the time would arrive when I would stop watching the clock and would become so caught up in the music I would never know how long I'd been practicing. And the fact of the matter is the method worked and I came to love playing the trumpet. And yet I suppose parents will be getting uptight about meditation; they won't see it as the same kind of thing as eating carrots or playing the trumpet.

The parents will be baffled. They will ask, why would my son want to do some peculiar thing like this meditation? When their son tries to explain it seems worth trying because he learned at his mother's knee to eat carrots and swallow vitamin pills and practice the violin just because she guaranteed these things would work for his good—will we have to go through the whole generational gap over this bit? Perhaps we need to choose the metaphors more precisely, because all understanding and all misunderstanding is wrapped up with memories of fears and pleasures, rather than with any present essence. No parent can react to the idea of meditation, or to marijuana, just at the mention of the word; the reaction has to be tied to some repellent image of a weird, foreign cult, or to a damp jail cell—conjured up more likely from bad movies than any real recall.

When you're driving on a long trip there is lots of time to reminisce, and we did. At one point we were passing a long line of telephone poles and as they flashed by, flicking at me, my mind was triggered to a time when I was small and walked beside a long iron fence. I had a stick and as I walked I struck one rung and the stick was bounced to the next, building up a small tattoo. I often walked that block and I loved to strike the metal fence rails. The rhythmic repetition of the sound and of the feeling, telegraphed to my fingers, acted in some way to make a hum that blanked out any other distractions and my mind was set free of conscious boredom. I became free of care and I would not even be aware of the banal pattern of the metallic sound. I would lift off into childish fantasy, very likely forget completely I was being sent to the store on an errand. I don't think it is important for people to remember their childhood day-dreams but it is important they recall the feeling of these dreams, the participation in bliss, rather than identify with one single aspect of it.

Meditation was a subject we spent hours explaining to ourselves, trying to see if we could arrive at an explanation which would seem reasonable to someone (some "official") who was ready to add it to the list of "dangerous" things the younger generation is experiencing. First, it would be necessary to make clear meditation is not an austere pursuit of the divine. Any "official" knows you go to a proper church if you care about that kind of thing. It is not a colorful affectation or mannerism. Probably people all over the world everywhere meditate without ever calling it by that name, in some of the least likely settings: sitting on a bench, whittling; perhaps kneeling, with a rosary in the fingers. Are not repeated "Hail Mary's" similar to the Indian mantras, which are simply a few syllables, repeated and repeated in the beginning of a meditation period in order to set up a freeing pattern like my childhood fence syllables? What the mantra achieves is probably very much like what mowing the lawn, knitting, running, bicycling, or practicing a musical instrument does for some people. What passes for "loafing"—the act of fishing with no particular catch in mind, say—is a closely related device to free the mind to go where it will.

Maharishi stresses the importance of meditating regularly;

this means doing it morning and evening for a few minutes. One should also be left undisturbed and alone. Parents might understand the discipline in this; it is like brushing your teeth regularly, practicing the piano regularly, even saying prayers regularly. Nobody believes that you ever make up lost time by brushing your teeth all day Sunday if you failed to brush them during the week. Would it ever get to the level of a Senate subcommittee hearing? If some "official" matches up his list of known, convicted marijuana users with a membership list of Meditation Society members—and finds, as he just might, a correlation—the day may dawn when Maharishi has to come clean to Senator Dodd. I can hear Agent Parnetta adding his invective; he would find meditation pretty vicious, I think; you wouldn't get him to stop at the point of thinking it just spooky or sinister.

We asked *ourselves,* why meditation? . . . all of a sudden? . . . now? We speculated it might be the result of the vanishing adolescence sociologists have been warning us about for years. Since the Sputnik (and the Edsel!) our schools have become increasingly intense. I was told in grade school I would probably never amount to anything— I'd never survive junior high even, unless I concentrated more and more and got better grades, and, and . . . The warnings proliferated until in prep school the instruction and the warnings shared about equal time. It doesn't really ever let up any more if you have your ears tuned to hear.

We bought a *New Yorker* magazine and Al read aloud from a piece about Dr. Jerome Lettvin, professor of communications physiology at the Massachusetts Institute of Technology. He was described as six feet tall, weighing two hundred and seventy pounds. Although he works in the Research Laboratory of Electronics he is an M.D. who is now devoting his time to a study of student drug addiction. Lettvin is one of the enlightened older generation, as disturbed as the students are about the mood and the style of their education. He says, "Education has become a shopkeeper's edu-

cation—a competition to get into college, in which schools
have become businesses, rather than refuges from the world;
in which ideas, as ideals, have been devalued, and in which
one kid is set against another as a potential enemy. There is
no room for the scholar. The children have been driven to
ask what the purposes of education are. Most of them don't
want to have anything to do with it. The situation has been
made critical by the abominable treatment of the Negro . . .
Some of the best minds have turned against science as being
responsible for it [the Vietnam war]. Science is being re-
jected because of its fruits. Every part of the teacher suffers
with these kids. There is blood on the hands of all of us. This
is terrifying. The moral and ethical aspects of the world
have intruded so that to practice science is like painting with
a toothache. It's a moral ache. So I'm staying with the kids,
instead of concentrating on research, and I'm devoting a lot
of time to supporting Senator McCarthy in order to defeat
the present tyranny that we're under." Sounds great, but I'll
bet admissions standards at MIT, Lettvin's school, are still
geared to the values he is railing against, the values which
trap the parents into pressuring their kids from childhood
on. And I'll bet students are expelled from his school if they
are picked up on a marijuana offense.

Some parents are heard to complain that their children's
lives are so programmed and scheduled and motivated and
directed, there is no time for the periods they recall from
their youth when kids were free to spend hours at random,
even daydreaming as they walked by picket fences. Saturday
is no longer an incredibly wonderful day with unknown and
delicious possibilities. Saturday for too many kids is a music
lesson, followed by a trip to the orthodontist, followed by
Little League practice, followed by a planned family get-
together, etc. But the same parents who bemoan this high
pressure on their kids usually continue to go right along with
the system. It would be cruel to call the parents hypocritical.
The worst they are is protective. They feel the hard com-
petitiveness of the world will crush their kids unless the kids

are armed with degrees from good schools. That degree had better certify that Junior is a well-trained, skilled expert in some good field (anyone for "plastics"?) if not in one of the standard professions. Junior better bite the bullet in school and he'd better be ready to bite on real ones pretty soon in Vietnam—if not in Vietnam, then on some other soon-to-arrive battlefield.

So the kids are finally on their own in college, which pleases the parents exactly in proportion to the reputation of the college. And which apparently displeases the kids in the same proportion. Because the best colleges in the country, the ones with the highest admissions standards, contain more disillusioned students than those with less stringent requirements.

We drove into Riverside, California, and bought a newspaper there. We learned that Bates Lowry, a former faculty member of the University of California at Riverside, had delivered a lecture the night before on "The Collapse of the Ivory Tower." He said the college there provided an excellent case study for understanding the development of today's educational dilemma. "Many [of the faculty] had been chosen for their commitment to the idea of a liberal arts college, but gradually the emphasis on forming a curriculum with a strong core of required studies shifted to a curriculum which favored the development of professional schools and graduate work—a change brought about by the pressure of the physical scientists . . . The dismal fact is that the opportunity for college students to work in general courses of any true depth as well as breadth has been drastically diminished." He suggested scholars and critics need a place from which to view society from afar—a place from which they could occasionally shout warnings to those below about what might lie ahead. Lowry is the newly appointed director of the Museum of Modern Art in New York City. MOMA is one of the favorite places for my generation; Al and I could look at each other and just smile, thinking of afternoons we'd spent there. We agreed we liked Lowry's being there rather than having him stay on in the faculty at Riverside. Lowry had a lot of good things to say. He talked about young people entering college with a vast set of sensory, intellectual, and moral impressions from TV—including a keen awareness of contradictory double standards, much more so than their pre-TV ancestors. I wonder if parents think much about the way in which TV educates their kids in that one sense alone? Kids are subjected, said Lowry, to multiple-choice exams instead of discussions, and they had identified themselves with new hopes that reject a simple check-off answer. "For this group's experience of our society, I do not think we can underestimate the impact of the brutal assassination of President Kennedy and the subsequent events. The college curricula have become shaped by this preparatory role so that the courses have become increasingly laden with information rather than thought-provoking . . . We must re-introduce courses which deal with the material that encourages students to evaluate their experiences in human terms." (*Pace* JFK; move over, here comes Martin Luther King, with your brother right behind him.)

It seemed to us, as we drove along, everything we heard or read or thought tied in with everything else. Lowry never said anything about meditation but we felt he would understand what it was all about and why. For while Junior is meditating he is not defining himself as a musician, ball player, even-toothed smiler, most-likely-to-succeeder. Perhaps if meditation can provide a chance for undefined self-illumination, self-exploration, some of the alienation between the generations will vanish. The child who left his nice home in Cincinnati to go live in Haight-Ashbury was mainly saying he could not live within the definition his parents set for him; and they would not tolerate his head-butting against the walls of their definition. Usually the parents would add to their side of the argument that the child didn't *really* know what he wanted anyway. The parents would be right on that score; but they would be wrong in thinking the child had to be boxed into their definition meanwhile or until he found his own measure. Because the child *knows* he can't find out what he might do, feel, think about any number of things if he is kept in a box.

Schools have been mainly boxes, or better yet, to use their own terminology, like tracks. If you seem like college material and you have even a faintly clean-cut look, and you do well in sports, you are expected to keep right on functioning in that style. If you want to experiment with some courses which don't fit the college-bound track you haven't a chance. If you decide to wear your hair longer the coach will be all over you. If you take the next step, and quit the team, and you were worth anything at all on it, everybody will be all over you. So you are expected to outgrow all habits which do not fit the image; it is like making the pan fit the pie. You are asked to reject many notions without even trying them. Once I wanted to experiment with an art course but it was scheduled during the band period and having proved I could play the trumpet I was expected to stick with that and demonstrate consistent, applied effort in one direction. Counselors, parents, teachers will even say they themselves think it would be nice to let you try some other things, sometimes, but the point is the good college (where you surely want to go) demands thus and so, and therefore, sad to relate, the student had better focus in and stay right there and accumulate an ideal consistent record—keep on the track.

Not surprisingly it sounds like the argument I kept hearing about marijuana; it may well be it is not harmful but the law is the law is the law . . . In an older generation one could run away to sea, work on a tramp steamer, or just bum around the world, trying out oneself, defining oneself. It was considered suitable and appropriate for young men not to be under their parents' scrutiny during such a period. It is very hard, if not impossible, for most young people to do that now. Even if your parents would permit it, the labor unions and the draft boards would not. Leaves of absence must be programmed and scheduled; there are miles of forms.

to be filled out if you do so much as a junior year abroad, not to mention the Peace Corps. You may get away, but only within a tighter embrace. The only community which beckons a young person and offers some kind of shelter, with no questions asked, is the hippie community. Within a larger society, which hates and fears it, this refuge is fast disappearing.

Some of our friends had survived hippiedom and they had graduated into all sorts of interesting endeavors, making beautiful things and selling those beautiful things. Some of them made beautiful music and sold it. Some parents were known to forgive when the sales mounted to an impressive figure. I told Al about Ian's dream of a farm in Virginia. We had several friends who had left the cities to go back to the land. Some of them were high-school dropouts; some of them were college dropouts; others went the whole route, including the military, even tried the "straight" world for a few years and then departed. (We read in a newspaper that Lindbergh had surfaced to address a conservationist group in Alaska; the item went on to say that Lindbergh's son was a rancher in Montana. In a recent speech, Lindbergh said, "If I were entering adulthood now instead of years ago, I would choose a career that kept me in contact with nature more than science. This is a choice an individual still can make—but no longer mankind in general.") Some of our generation have learned to love a life far away from the cities. Others try it and return to the cities more despairing than when they left.

The radio chipped in a comment, reporting a federal inspection of packages mailed to the U.S. from Vietnam had uncovered large amounts of marijuana in many of the packages. We wondered what laws would apply to this kind of international incident. Are the mailee and the mailer both felons? Especially when it is a package coming from a country where the contents are OK? Also, they found what they had first set out to look for, quantities of ammunition and thousands of weapons being sent home, perhaps for this summer's games? The radio told us the National Guard now stood shoulder to shoulder around the White House. Where did we stand? Only the extremists, black or white, could easily find their places. In the middle, there might be a place to balance. In the middle is where you lived through it—thinking your own best or worst thoughts. There is not much action in the middle . . . lots of time for meditation. Was meditation an escape into oneself? What other way is there to go? If you can't rush out to the barricades, where do you go? Ivory towers belong to another time; our generation won't ever reconstruct universities or churches as refuges. The haven will be right where we are if it's anywhere.

We blew a lot of bubbles, intellectually and really. Maharishi likes to use a bubble metaphor: thoughts are like bubbles in the ocean. They start as tiny specks of air in the deeps and gradually grow larger as they rise to the surface of our waking consciousness, on the most gross level of experience. Meditation takes us to the source of the thought-bubble in the deepest region of consciousness, the finest and first levels of experience.

We examined a lot of everyday paradoxes as the radio set Washington on fire for us. Had burning been certified as a properly defiant gesture in our father's time? Had it anything to do with burning out the Japanese with flame-throwers in World War II and napalming villages and tunnels in Vietnam? Maybe it was a throwback to ancient, primitive fire rituals, or maybe it was just the cheapest, handiest way to raise hell when some kind of urge to action wells up and there is no satisfactory, socially approved way to release the pent-up, mixed-up feelings. A riot "official" in *U.S. News and World Report* says the urban war is caused by a mixture of those and many other feelings. The rioters include a small percentage of activists, a few Communists, a smattering of hippies hung up with the generational gap, some pro-war types who don't think the United States is fighting hard enough in Vietnam, some anti-war types who feel just the opposite, some idle types who go along with whatever action offers excitement. Makes it sound like the makeup of a baseball crowd. Except that predominantly in this mix, in all categories, would be the frustrated Negroes: employed and unemployed, war veterans and defense-plant veterans, mostly young, acting out their combined confusions. The result is not revolution, but insurrection, and it will be treated as such.

In the Army news broadcasts in Vietnam we used the word "insurgency" rather often. The British advisers, skilled in counterinsurgency from their victorious campaigns in Malaysia, urged very specific search-and-destroy tactics for Vietnam. But the infiltration of the Viet Cong was infinitely more daring and also more subtle than the Communist-inspired infiltration in Malaysia. The result was the prolonged no-win for either side which dismayed people everywhere. The U.S. troops were trained very carefully to promote insurgency where that policy would apply and counterinsurgency where that was indicated. The net result provided thousands of American troops with very technically advanced understanding of the best ways to conduct guerrilla warfare in almost any situation—in cities or out in the country. This will be highly adaptable for domestic use when the veterans return to civilian status, therefore very special measures are being taken to defuse these soldiers.

After World War II there were many soldiers who needed some hospitalization before they were pronounced ready to adapt to civilian life. But it is a special feature of the Vietnam conflict that carefully devised training is considered necessary to untrain the United States soldiers before they are pronounced OK. Nearly all of them would have had only a year in Vietnam, unlike the World War II duties which often kept soldiers attached to a battlefront for much longer periods. I wondered if the training is considered successful and how many ex-soldiers had been put through it by now. Did our masterminds think it necessary for both white and Negro soldiers? Probably there would be more concern to pacify and rehabilitate the Negro returnees. Would it be brainwashing or soul-washing? Maybe it could be handled on a purely physiological basis and become as mechanical and as effective as the first crash program the soldier is put through when he is in basic training. Or—as mechanical and as effective as meditation. I wondered if the act of setting fire to a building can be felt as a kind of washing for the arsonist. Are the fires right now being set by veterans from last year's fires or does this necessarily involve new people? Since all soldiers have had to live with the contradiction that murder for the flag is different from murder impromptu, is there any new aspect with the returning veterans having at least walk-on parts? Those veterans would bring their special experience with intimate domestic engagements where a village is destroyed by the right hand and rebuilt by the left.

This was the crux of Dr. Levy's case: he refused to train Green Beret forces in the medical arts because the contradiction was impossible for him to bear—and now he's in jail for his pains. Dr. Levy is one of the rare members of any generation who felt his commitment (in his case to the healing arts) was so strong and so integrated into his personality that he would not, could not, violate it, by teaching medicine to soldiers who in reality would have to use it for political ends. His brief flurry in the news passed off into history because there is not time to examine anything so basic in a time of war. It amounts to treason when individual interests are pitted against national interests. The point of Dr. Levy's dilemma is that he was faced with only two alternatives: he could acquiesce to the Army, teach some of his medical skills to the warriors, or he could refuse, be adjudged an insurrectionist, and be put in jail. The rioting Negroes likewise have only two alternatives that seem real to them: they can acquiesce to what seems to them an interminably slow improvement of their condition, or they can turn insurrectionist and strike out with riots and burning.

The white folks would approve the first course; the second

course would be treated as nihilistic anarchy. But the third course, the really good revolutionary change that is desired, does not seem possible—any realistic white or Negro knows this. Under present conditions the desirable changes are going to take a long, long time. No matter how many peace talks and peace moves are made in Asia, the effort there in dollars and sensibility will not be detoured completely into our cities. Visible justice and adequate fulfillment for the Negro in America is going to take a long, long time. Faced with that fact, and confident there are not enough jails to hold them all, the Negroes find relief in burning up their environment. They are certainly bringing tears to Martin Luther King in his celestial preserve, because he was such a moral man, brimming with concern for the rights and wrongs of society. Probably he would understand, as well as anyone, though, that nobody will stand still while rights are established on an inch-by-inch basis. It is the nature of modern man, in America or elsewhere, to believe in perfectibility. This pushes him to impatiently want results in his own time, right now. If there is not a viable course for this urge to take it rushes out of control, floods its banks and wreaks destruction. All the impressive steps which have been taken in this century to improve society throughout the world only make the river run faster.

Dr. Levy's dilemma has few counterparts in Vietnam. There the ordinary draftees are quite accustomed to the contradiction of wearing two hats. They have been trained to combine, almost simultaneously, the skills of war and peace. They might spend half a day killing Vietnamese and half a day building a shelter for the orphans left after the battle. This contradiction is less difficult to stomach for the Negroes, raised in a morass of American contradictions, than it is for the white soldiers. The result will surely be dramatic. The Negroes can go the next step and use this contradiction; the white soldier is more apt to be used up by the awfulness of it—if he lets himself think about it at all. The Negro can come home now, feeling stronger for his Army hitch, and see that he can do some of the same contradictory things in his own neighborhood. If, someday soon, Americans think it *just* that the Viet Cong may have prevailed against the might of America, it will probably be *equally just* that the American Negro found his rightful place in American society by taking advantage of the same tactics.

We speculated about the militant newly graduated college students, 150,000 strong, headed for the draft. If you add their girl friends and wives to that figure, and the sympathetic students who are going into their senior year, there will be quite an army. Is there an original or extraordinary statement left for them to make? We have already absorbed incidents where blood was poured into Selective Service files and individuals burned themselves alive. We have an amazing capacity to know about such things, to examine photographs of the event, and to move our attention on to the next event. This student army will have to wrack its brains to invent a truly meaningful gesture which Americans cannot shrug off within a day or two. No doubt there are many plans being considered, rehearsed, and coordinated. Al and I agreed if the students smoked marijuana while they made their plans there would be very few carried out. The establishment would be well advised to postpone their daily "busts"; marijuana might be the best ally the police ever had. All the classic passive-resistance moves have been made (sit-ins, lie-ins, marches, rallies, etc.) ad infinitum. These things have a certain nobility but the impatient activists have learned noble moves earn noble replies—and little more. The democratic ritual promises reform later on; current dissensus demands society be remade right now. The furious young whites have learned so much from the Negroes' efforts; like Chuang-tzu's frog in the well, the Negroes were denied knowledge of the outside world for so long they want to jump out right now—even if they perish in the process. The students are more like Wittgenstein's fly in the fly-bottle—buzzing angrily and at any moment apt to find there is no stopper

in the bottle. Having once seen the opening, the rioting Columbia students jammed the neck of the bottle in hopes that a few would get out. Of course those who got out might find they are in a room, and in time they'll discover the door out of the room is open . . . except that it seems blocked by a semitransparent cordon of policemen trying to make their escape in the other direction.

We returned to an earlier theme which had served to support us in prep school—the idea based on there being two alternatives, the shitty and the wonderful. A school counselor had tried to cope with one of my depressions by agreeing with me that everything may well seem shitty, but by nurturing and fostering my ability to rationalize, he showed me how it could also be wonderful sometimes. The third thing, the hardest thing to learn, was that we all lived and died in spite of those extremes and that living is most meaningful somewhere in between. In fact, because of extremes you are going to have to work out a middle course if you care about health, peace, happiness. Meanwhile our culture keeps throwing us curves which are usually shitty or wonderful and we have an agonizingly difficult time trying to stay in the middle or even find where the middle is. It is a lot easier to find either of the extremes. *Viz.* American politics in 1968.

We agreed that meditation, extreme as it may sound, is probably a shorter path to the middle than any other route one might take. But we also knew many college students would never have believed in the possibility if they had been introduced to it when they were cold sober. The mind-expanding, door-opening experiences of an assortment of sensual and chemical stimulation had to have taken place first before most students would believe that bliss (fluctuating somewhere near the middle if it is anywhere) even existed.

When the radio palled we shoved a cartridge into the stereo tape deck built right into our road module and we were flooded with the nostalgic bath of sensual stimulation our generation accepted as normal. Far cry from coming across these plains in a covered wagon, eh? We sketched a profile of Chuck Somebody, allowing him all of the luxuries we had had in our respective youths and a few extra ones we had craved. Chuck had soaked up thousands of hours of rich music from the time he was born. His father had strangled at the thought but Chuck was given a very good transistor radio when he was in grade school and he carried it with him wherever he went. Very soon he had his own TV and stereo in his room. It was part of his natural environment. He had a motorbike when he was in his early teens and a sports car by the time he was in high school. Chuck experimented with sex, and beer, and cigarettes in junior high—also sniffed a little glue. It was all part of exploring the things which made him feel different from the everyday way he felt. Not everyone in his school shared his interests but he knew so many bright, curious, imaginative ones who did, that he felt in no way special.

In high school Chuck carried out his explorations further with marijuana, and then at one party he was introduced to LSD. Acid was perfectly legal then and someone from Los Angeles had brought down a sack of sugar cubes, each soaked in the stuff. You could get it in many coffeehouses in Los Angeles, San Francisco, Boston, New York with no trouble at all. Bowls of these sugar cubes were on the coffee counters in many places. Chuck's first acid trip opened up possibilities far beyond all the other things he'd tried so far. He didn't give up any of the other things—each one had its place and each one provided a certain kind of stimulation or release. He used these devices very rarely because he studied hard and got good grades—that was a particular kind of trip, too. He read widely, dabbling his toes in religion, politics, sports, astrology, sex—anything and everything offered some kind of flavor that tickled the senses and he expected to have his senses perpetually responding. He played the guitar quite well and he built a rocket (with a group sponsored by NASA) and he held an office in student government and he had a steady girl and only a few traffic tickets. He had no feeling he was "on drugs" at all, and he wasn't. He had sampled some of his parents' medical prescriptions with their approval when he needed to go to sleep and couldn't (after a hard day at school) or when he had to stay up late (to study for an exam), but this was rare.

Chuck was headed for a good college and each day put him one step closer to that goal. He knew the word "absurd" because as a senior in high-school English he had to read and discuss briefly a few authors like Camus. Holden Caulfield's concern with the "phoniness" of middle-class society was comfortably tucked into Chuck's mental bag and it didn't bother him much—the idea was *passé*. Chuck was so busy with each day's imperatives that he was happy to postpone any heavy thinking until some later date. In general, he was quite socially approved and he never talked much about meaning or direction or purpose in a long-range perspective. He was a good kid and his parents didn't begrudge him what his toys cost them.

During his freshman year he began to use words like "absurd" and "mindless" and "ludicrous" in a new way. All sorts of things he had looked at without seeing were suddenly visible and had to be questioned. There were a few answers available to him; in the summer he went South and marched for civil rights. He came back to school pretty fired up about the abuse of the Negro and he joined a group of activists on the campus who were really taking positive steps in this issue. He ended up very puzzled when he was accused of being a bigot and a racist by a black-power Negro, because there were so few Negroes at Chuck's school. Chuck didn't want to be patronizing but when he volunteered, in reply, that he had roomed with a Negro boy that summer he was greeted with both sneers and laughter. Chuck got the point but it was cold comfort.

He lived through a lot of days without any sense of commitment. Philosophy and psychology courses fed him more

G

information; he had a big vocabulary and a lot of information. He talked to college seniors and got little encouragement there. Mostly they were completing requirements for their majors, much as they would chop up wood for a fire. They told him the action was all really going to happen in some post-doctoral nirvana. And this seemed probable because the graduate students (most of Chuck's teachers—the ones who knew his name—were graduate students) wrapped themselves up in nitpicking scholarly games. Those getting a degree in philosophy were so tied up with solving linguistic puzzles that "meaning" was out to lunch. The physical- and the social-science people were absorbed in measuring things with their new computer-toys. The fraternity boys, who were obviously going to become pillars of the establishment when they graduated, handled their dilemmas by getting drunk very religiously (with or without girls) on the weekends and filling in all the cracks during the week with high-stake card games. Chuck tried that scene for a whole term, thinking it might be at least a soporific. One of his father's friends had given him the word just before he left home for college: join a good fraternity, hold your liquor, play bridge well, and don't borrow money from your friends. The students who best fit the academic design seemed not to ask questions, or at least they specialized in asking the kind for which there were neat answers. They could sail through the whole undergraduate storm without pain if they would settle for information. Many of them did.

Chuck's fate was to be alive during a steadily affluent period. Affluence means many more choices are open; when you have a lot of choices you can afford to look them all over. You run the risk of not liking any of them, of course. Chuck tried politics and sociology because that was where most of the humanists congregated: there were clubs devoted to various hero-gurus, ranging from Che Guevara to Ayn Rand. The student political activists seemed enviable to Chuck because their life and their minds appeared filled to the brim— no voids. He audited quite a lot of graduate lectures and he was stimulated from time to time by certain men who would drop in for a lecture once or twice a year. In between he could read their books and be intrigued by their ideas, and he did just that, but it was far away from where he was at the moment. The best times were those he spent with students who related to the arts in some way. Their rooms were ingeniously decorated; their ideas were playfully spontaneous; their attitudes about life and school were more creative; their conventions were few.

Chuck still studied enough to get by but he was increasingly uncertain about what he was doing at school except going through a lot of prescribed motions, much as he had gone through all the grades which led him there. If most of the outside world seemed absurdly futile at best and wickedly cruel at worst, maybe the answer was to be found inside himself. The few people he brushed against in books or in life, who appeared poised, seemed to be fed from inner sources rather than from society. Chuck had had a few sessions with the college psychiatrist. He (and the psychiatrist) felt pretty certain Chuck was not any more disturbed than most other people and he actually wasn't. What to do while waiting for commitment to reveal itself? He knew from several years of acquaintance that liquor made him behave differently from his everyday behavior but it was mainly a blanking-out kind of effect —no insights were provided. Marijuana made him feel relaxed and ready to forgo insights peacefully. He could use liquor, marijuana, pep pills, tranquilizers, even vitamins, to alter his consciousness or the way he felt, and thus he was enabled, when he felt shitty, to add some element and feel better—maybe even, for a while, to feel wonderful. He never felt enormously altered, of course. Chuck and some of his friends discovered about the same time that the scope of their character was what made anything shitty or wonderful. Somehow, in the twentieth century this was a timely relief. In spite of the abounding contradictions of society he could at least know that within the shitty was the same self that could create and be the wonderful. If he had to forget the good it was only temporarily. Knowing this was not quite enough for Chuck, although when he talked about this once to the psychiatrist he was told that he was really progressing. He tried to explain the idea to his parents and they thought he was getting into pretty deep stuff and they told each other that Chuck was going to be OK and they hoped he would stop there. His parents' concern was well founded. When Chuck talked to them in this vein it was true that he was not through pursuing his self-doubts and his self-inquiry.

Chuck used acid about a dozen times, usually on long weekends when he had time to take a trip without ruining his study schedule. When he was growing up, at home, with his consciousness soothed, provoked, or titillated by all his toys, he never actually thought about his consciousness. He just sat in the middle of his stereo speakers or rode his bike because it felt good. Sex was very much the same thing, although there were odds and ends of other overtones there—which he pushed away from his mind at this time. He didn't think his personal quest had much to do with satisfying his sexual appetite, and he was right about that. He knew that sex and love were two different things, but he felt that he couldn't really love anybody until he came to some better terms with himself. After acid he *knew* he had consciousness and everything about it was more real than any of his toys had been, more real than sex had ever been, and much, much more interesting than school.

Acid opened doors in his mind that he hadn't known existed, let alone what was behind the doors. Perhaps, in another generation, he would have stumbled on these doors when he bummed around the world, but with acid he could sit right down in his room and take the trip. Perhaps, in another generation, he would have arrived at the same place with religion, psychotherapy—or even from a deeper involvement with education at his own school. The point was that he had been exposed to some of those things and none of them grabbed him and opened up the inside of his head to himself the way acid did. Inside his head he found no answers to the questions which had plagued him—What should his major be? Are the existing jobs in the world worth filling? Why compete to get ahead when most of the people who are ahead seem to have only ulcers? But he did have a heightened sense of himself as a valuable human being and he had a new feeling of being at home with himself in a very basic, elementary way he thought he had never experienced before. Perhaps he may have felt easy in his skin when he was a baby but for years he had been feeling the world was tight around him.

He talked about acid with some of his friends. Very few shared Chuck's sense of personal quest. One of his artist friends felt that an acid trip mainly led him to fantastically exciting graphic patterns. Some non-artists shared that opinion, and they hugely enjoyed the visual stimulation. A pre-med boy reported acid let him understand why cells develop. A business administration major thought he now had insights into human nature which would make him immensely successful—and rich.

Some students went around claiming new insights into many things they had read in the past. A history major, after acid, wrote a thesis on Francis Bacon's thought: "The contemplation of things as they are without error or confusion, without substitution or imposture, is in itself a nobler thing than a whole harvest of invention." Perhaps the same thought would have appealed to him before acid, but the student said it would not have. Chuck's girl friend, after acid, phoned him one night to say now she really understood what Gertrude Stein meant when she said, "It is not so much what France gives you as what it doesn't take away."

Some students were able to verbalize a special kind of kinship which acid produced; for example, listening to music, while on acid, made them feel a part of the musician and a part of the very music itself. Sitting on the beach they reported feeling as if they were a part of the waves that rushed up to their feet, or inside the body of a seagull that flew overhead. Chuck shared many similar feelings, but his area of interest was not specifically defined, and he wondered if he was Somebody in the sense that he belonged to an intellectual campus elite rather above most of the other students. But as his mind opened up farther he concluded that everybody was Somebody—he was not necessarily more intelligent than or inherently superior to the newsvendor on the corner. This feeling came to him with pleasure; there was no sense of loss as he assimilated this idea. In fact, it came to him as a very agreeable idea. He said "Everyone should do his thing" with new understanding, because he knew people were richly various and would remain so.

Before acid, logic had been organized on a step-by-step basis of cause and effect. He would find something irritating; he would decide to be angry; then he would be uncomfortable being angry. The adrenalin coursing through his system would have him so jammed up, the emotion would have to run its course. Later, he would have to rationalize his way back step by step to an understanding of what had made him angry. After acid, his chemically governed logic was supplanted with what felt like an intuitive realization that he didn't have to get angry at all. He was much freer to choose whether to be angry or not—he was not as reactive as he had been. He could experience the full range of emotions but he was not blocked and constricted into anxious, guilt-ridden crises. He was free to surmount his problems by accepting the fact they were there rather than rejecting or fighting them. Chuck read the Chinese philosophy of Wu Wei with new understanding. He had taken some judo lessons and he understood the principle of using the thrust of an attack as a force with which to divert the attack. He knew that he turned the wheel of his car into the skid rather than against it. Now he consciously could use that law in all manner of situations.

He tried to think back to when things had first become constricting. It seemed to him that somewhere in early childhood he had embarked on a road of learning, involvement, achievement, and for years he hadn't thought much about being at home with himself. He had come to think of himself as other people thought about him, in terms of what was measurable in age, feet, pounds, grades, awards, possessions. Beyond those tangibles he thought he might be only a collection of affectations and mannerisms acquired by reacting to his own reactions. Was there a center on which all the outward signs hung? He had become increasingly suspicious there was a void at his center which could never be filled. Acid taught him the superficial things he knew about himself did surround a void: untouchable, unfindable, unknowable. Yet the void had a solidarity which brought all the flimsier aspects into the perspective of his personality. He had no sense it was filled with anything substantial because the heart of the meaning was undetermined. He was not puzzled by this; he accepted it as readily as he accepted the idea that his finger could never touch its own tip.

Chuck had long discussions with a friend who had recently become a convert to Catholicism after using acid. They both agreed no matter what words were used, the happiest moments in life had always eluded precise definition. The Catholic boy had taken for his motto: "Everybody sees what you appear to be; few feel what you are." Just as light could not be known in itself but rather by what it illuminated, the two boys could not agree on the words to express the discoveries which were going to change their whole lives—but the discoveries, as the boys, were nonetheless real. They could agree the mind was the intangible void through which all things worked and they hugely enjoyed sharing this idea.

Al and I were competing at this point for the privilege of adding the next touch to the enlightenment of Chuck. He had started out as a figment of our imagination but now we felt as if he were riding along with us in the car. Al added the next bit. He suggested that Chuck felt the bottomless pool of his sentient self was truly "the way" . . . Lao-tzu's "mother of all things." Together we chanted: Chuck was subject to the laws of the world, the world was subject to the laws of the universe, the universe was subject to the laws of the Tao, and the Tao was subject to the laws of its own nature.

Al quickly added the next line: "Chuck's mind is the Tao!" I contributed, "At once like a turning wheel, a clay bowl— a 'Preface to God!'"

We had both read Michael Polanyi (chemist-turned-philosopher) and we debated whether his more Western view might not put the intangible hierarchy the other way around: the conscience controls intelligence, intelligence controls movement, movement controls the elements given us through the play of our mind. To use Polanyi's metaphor, it was as if Chuck had been using a stick to feel his way in the dark. Before, he had been hung up with the feeling of holding the stick firmly in his hand. Now he could shift his attention to the end of the stick where it touched a rock in his path. Before, he had gripped the stick so tightly and strained so hard he stumbled over every rock in the path. Now, imagination and understanding flowed back and forth through the stick. His mind created what it experienced and experienced what it created. Simultaneously, as thoughts poured out of a bottomless spring, the mind was manufacturing its own time and space to hold them. Chuck felt his way in the dark rather well now. Unspecifiable expectations made him look to the future with a new openness.

But acid was expensive, perhaps dangerous, and definitely exhausting—even if it was great. Chuck was not sold on acid as a way of life and he was ready now, as he hadn't been before, to consider some other, better ways to achieve this feeling of self-understanding. Before acid he would not have cared much about a lecture on Eastern religion, for example. Now he was opened up to the possibilities that any activity, any direction, might provide fruits which were edible. When he heard that Maharishi had some way of showing you how to involve your consciousness, all by yourself, Chuck was ready for that. At once, hearing Maharishi speak, he was on his way. He knew he would not become new in any startling fashion. He would still be chasing illusive answers, but he would not feel so trapped by the questions. He felt no dependency on drugs of any kind. To be sociable he would smoke marijuana or take a drink, but these were not things he would go off and do by himself. He was essentially the same Chuck but now he was more aware. He did not vacillate from the extremes of thinking everything was either shitty or wonderful. He was joyful about some things; cautious about others. He was ready for action in a mindful as well as a mindless way.

He tried to explain this to his parents and they followed him up to a point but they told him they expected college alone would have produced this effect—in fact, they rather hoped it would. But when Chuck talked about chemical and spiritual and biological and metaphysical levels they were worried. They expressed concern that Chuck might have damaged himself in some permanent way with acid. They had read reports of acid causing broken chromosomes. Of course, chromosomes broke all the time, anyway . . . but how much? How many? Did acid do more damage than the medical drugs that most people use? More than dental X rays? What about other radiation? What about that nerve gas that killed all the sheep? What might happen to children born of mothers exposed to acid or nerve gas? What about Chuck's unborn children? It reminded them of that summer when Chuck had bicycled all over Europe. They had worried about everything from flat tires to volcanic eruptions. If Chuck had had their ability to imagine the worst he could never have started on the trip—let alone enjoyed it.

Chuck went to a lecture one evening with his parents and heard Professor Herbert Marcuse (of very distinguished age and intellectual achievements) say that he couldn't imagine an intelligent and sincere man who did not feel that opposition to this society was a necessity on many levels, and in many terms—not just for political or philosophical reasons but even for moral and biological and chemical ones. Chuck's parents thought that was a lot to say about our society and they thought this professor seemed more shaken up by the world around him than Chuck had ever been. Maybe Chuck would be all right. Fortunately they read Henry Luce's biography not long after that and the parts which described the deeply rewarding acid trips which Claire and Henry took reassured them so they didn't worry specifically about acid any more. Chuck and his friends felt acid had done its thing and they were on to the next thing. Tim Leary's sideshows had helped them arrive at a natural moderation, which is what Dr. Leary intended in spite of himself. Chuck's younger brother in junior high was trying LSD; probably the whole idea was filtering out into nothing—a burst bubble. Just as Chuck had grown up believing in the power of democracy without conscious effort, maybe the next generation would grow up ready to believe in meditation. Until something better came along—and it *certainly* would. Already the Maharishi had seen an end to his world mission. Apparently he felt that he had failed in spreading the Word, his Word, a Word. He had given an immense boost to the idea of finding inside oneself the knowledge which makes for satisfactory living in the world. Before Freud we suspected the how-does-one-live question was answered mainly by dedication, resolve, ability—tempered, perhaps, by factors of possible circumstance or difficult sublimation. After Freud we were intoxicated with clearing out the interior traumas which constricted or distorted the inherent ability, resolve, *et al.* Post-Freudian adaptations and innovations have proliferated, synthesizing and categorizing from the partial successes along the way, preparing a path for something else. The Maharishi is one of a long line of holy men who turn up in history from time to time, serving to remind us that our answers and our questions are altogether inside each of us, like our talents and our traumas. Which is not to say that we may fatuously relax and just accept our situation whatever it may be. We must change and evolve constantly. But the growth will come from within our natures and it will be a flowering, not a manipulation, of ourselves. The way out is the way in. When Chuck came home one vacation, at about this time, his parents thought he had settled down a great deal; he seemed much more serious without being sad or morose. Our old Chuck, they said. Like Baudelaire's mirror, meditation was enabling him to become an enriched reflection of himself. Which is all anyone ever wanted in the first place.

We had become so absorbed with Chuck we weren't watching the map. A sign told us Los Alamos was coming up. On an impulse we decided to visit an old girl friend who lived in a small town quite near there. Of course she was home. Of course she was delighted to see us. (The ancient Greeks thought their gods controlled all continuity and fulfillment. The ancient Chinese thought it was synchronicity: every smallest act inexorably linked to the act before it— there was no coincidence, no chance, no impulse.) We were anxious to have a shower and get cleaned up. She offered an exotic solution. This part of the mountain country was dotted with hot springs. We hiked up a boulder-strewn trail for about a half a mile through tall evergreens, then pushed our way into a clearing and around a corner to find this amazing place. There was a stream of warm, clear, fresh water which trickled over the face of a big rock onto another huge rock below. The water had eroded the lower rock until it was a giant room-sized dish about four feet deep. The warm water overflowed and swirled down the mountain to join the Jemez River off in a valley. The trees thrust up all around the spring like the points of a crown. Remotely unfurling, the timbered mountains stretched eastward to the glittering alien prairies from where we'd come. Without our willing it we knew in the softest *déja vu* that we belonged here; we'd always been around. There was no sign whatever of any other human being. It was early evening and a light snow was falling. We stripped and the three of us jumped into the warm bath, splashing and frisking like seals. As darkness came on we lolled in the warm pool, feeling deliciously the primeval organisms which we were, at play in our natural environment. We were perfectly at home with our world round us,

as a Hindu saying puts it, like notes on one flute. It wasn't
to be known where the instrument stopped and the song
began. Mysteriously the music would always continue. The
snow kept falling, dropping straight down, closing in all
around us like a sheltering curtain, melting the instant it hit
the warm water.

APPENDIX I

SOME NOTES ON DRUGS

In America in the middle of the nineteenth century many thousands (mostly women) were developing addictions to the numerous patent medicines, like laudanum, made from opium derivatives; this was aggravated by the post–Civil War increase in morphine (hypodermically injected) addiction. To solve this state of affairs, in 1898 heroin (diacetyl-morphine) was made from morphine, which is, itself, made from an opium base, and was hailed as a "safe" medication, free from addictive properties. Physicians noted its opiate effects but it was regarded as a vast improvement over morphine, and became the favorite of the underworld drug traffic, for even though its euphoric qualities diminish and finally disappear after the first few months of use, there is a physical dependence which drives the addict to crave more and more simply to relieve the pain of abstinence or withdrawal. The heroin addict does not enjoy any "highs"; he only seeks relief from "lows." It is an interesting case of our clever technology pulling the roof in on our own heads.

Preliminary reports on an official Army study show that eighty-three per cent of soldiers questioned said that they had smoked marijuana. And on the same day that the chief U.S. Information Officer in Vietnam was calling Specialist Steinbeck's statement ridiculous, the Provost Marshal in

Saigon said that more servicemen were arrested for smoking marijuana than for any other offense. A new crackdown followed numerous press reports of this article, and a larger Army investigation has been launched.

It is interesting to note that Dr. Joel Fort, who is one of the nation's leading experts on drug abuse and a man who contributes copiously to the textbooks used by federal agencies to stem such abuse, lists marijuana, among other things, as a cure for alcoholism. In quoting crimes of violence, narcotic officials are always quick to point out that the Richard Specks are known to have had experience with marijuana. From there the officials make a quick step and put them into the same bag as the heroin users. This is done repeatedly, although the 1967 report of the President's Commission of Law Enforcement and the Administration of Justice has stated that there are not enough marijuana users who graduate to heroin or enough heroin users with a prior marijuana experience to substantiate any possible connection between the two. When this report says "not enough" I assume the amount must have been considerably less than fifty per cent, perhaps twenty-five per cent. However, if this line of reasoning is to be used and something less than *most* heroin users had prior marijuana experience how is one to regard the fact that *most* heroin users probably had prior experience with tobacco and alcohol?

Marijuana is used to help ease the withdrawal symptoms of hard-core heroin and morphine addicts. Tremendous success has historically been reported where marijuana is used in the treatment of schizophrenic and manic-depressive disorders, without the physical side effects of barbiturates and tranquilizers. An Army doctor friend told me the synthetic drugs being used in this field are still being prescribed with no real knowledge of their value. While I was in Vietnam this doctor was in charge of a psychiatric ward where Librium (a synthetic tranquilizer widely used in the United States) had been dispensed in vast quantities—passed out to the patients almost like salted nuts. Then an order had come in from stateside medical headquarters announcing that recent findings made it necessary to cease and desist this practice immediately and another synthetic was to be used in its place. The reputation of marijuana as a psychedelic or hallucinogenic has led to experiments with it as a remedy for the most widespread kind of psychological symptom, the oldest kind of anxiety, that of depersonalization, which means a disruption of one's concept of self—the feeling that the outside world is strange. In DeRopp's *Drugs and the Mind* there is a vivid case history of dramatic success in treating depersonalization with *Cannabis* extract.

The word "marijuana" is Spanish for a very poor grade of tobacco, and it was not the marijuana we think of today which developed such a legend throughout the East. But since the term is officially and legally used in the United States it has gathered to itself a kind of international acceptance. With the exception of the stalks and seeds of the hemp plant, most every other part contains a considerable amount of tetrahydrocannabinol alkaloid. When smoked this produces the characteristic effect. The seeds have to be baked or steamed to produce any effect. The most famous and touted product of the plant is hashish, also called dagga, charas, and majoun (a cookie with spices).

The coarse leaves of the plant, which are what is used mainly in the United States, are often thrown away in the Middle East. There they use only the finest flowering tops (as in the harvesting of tea leaves) and the pollen of the plants. The leaves come in many different grades—some of the very tiniest are selected, perhaps only two or three from each plant. A Persian acquaintance of mine described how most of the hashish that comes to this country is the lowest grade obtainable. The better quality grades are usually ordered before harvest and prepared according to the specifications of the wealthy Persian buyer with spices, perfumes, etc. This is reminiscent of the stories one hears about the finest French wine being saved and sold to certain special customers.

The Indonesian people never took the smoking of hemp to the sophisticated social levels that the Arabs, Indians, and Africans did. As a result, in Vietnam and Laos, and throughout most of Southeast Asia, marijuana (that is, the coarser, cruder leaves of the plant) is used as a mild daily panacea, rather than any kind of luxury. What hashish there is to be found in this part of Asia is not real hashish at all, but a concentrated version of the leaf made from the stickier flowering upper as well as lower parts of the plant. This smokable mass still looks like so many leaves and twigs, whereas the Mideastern variety of hashish is a dark-brown, black, dark-red, or green-and-yellow substance. It is a light shade when first collected because then it is the pure pollen. As it ages it darkens. At first it is a sticky powder (like most pollen), but this is compressed, whereupon it becomes like jam for some weeks and eventually hardens into a brick as hard as stone. A small pellet of the soft material could be smoked in a pipe, or added to a recipe. The taste of it in fudge, cookies, cake, etc. would be undetectable, but the effect would be to make one feel a bit lightheaded—similar to the effect of sparkling wine. Americans who are entertained abroad frequently eat hashish which is contained in some dish without realizing it. Wealthy Indians (who would shun alcohol) commonly serve canapés in which hashish is mixed with spicy pastes. Such a tidbit, sometimes decorated with fine shavings of real gold-leaf, is a delicacy that appears the way fine caviar would at a Russian feast.

When hashish is being harvested there must be immense fields of the plant to produce any quantity of the pollen. My Persian friend described the fields of mature plants, growing in immense acreage as we grow wheat. Years ago, when man-power was cheaper, the pollen was collected by having naked people run through the pollen-covered plants. The sticky pollen would attach itself to the bare skin, from which it could be scraped off. This method has been improved by using large leather aprons as collecting surfaces, and it seems likely that it would be more comfortable for the harvesters.

As Ashley Montagu, a well-known author and researcher, has pointed out, the worldwide search for certain substances which alter everyday reality has been going on forever in every part of the globe. One of the particular common denominators has been to hunt for and find those substances which contain alkaloids, because it is their release which provides the basic feeling of "comfort" which men seek. It is the alkaloids in tea, coffee, and chocolate which account for their popularity. Marijuana is not precisely the same but very similar in its chemical content. When chocolate was first developed commercially and was so immediately popular wherever people were exposed to it, a cacao boom took place in Brazil similar to the gold rush in the United States. One might suppose chocolate was just another agreeable flavor, but Montagu shows it was the alkaloid content, as with many other substances, which accounted for the international craving and appetite—not to mention price and profit involved. I remember the modern parents of a small boy who had arrived at the stage where his parents felt he needed enlightenment about sexual matters. They dutifully described everything which took place in order for small boys to be conceived. The child listened to all this and then inquired, "Do you get to eat chocolate while you're doing it?" He was already "hooked."

APPENDIX II

Mr. Chairman and members of the subcommittee:

I have agreed to give testimony today concerning use of the drug marijuana by service personnel in the Republic of Vietnam because I believe it is the sincere goal of this subcommittee to eventually arrive at a realistic view of the use of marijuana by Americans, a view unclouded by any particular moral opinion, to couple this view with modern scientific inquiry and then, with this information, to instigate whatever legislation best reflects public morality, civil rights and the national welfare.

None of this can be achieved without accurate information as to what marijuana is and especially what marijuana means to the people for whom the government would be passing any legislation. For it seems that the prohibition of a substance or the lack of such a prohibition involves the weight of public opinion far more than common sense or medical evidence.

The popular acceptance of cigarettes, while we know them

to be a health hazard, is an example. It is a medical fact that marijuana is far less harmful than the cancer-feeding tars contained in the everyday cigarette, which carries with it the very powerful addictive drug that is nicotine. Cigarette smoking, however, remains in the public domain of overall acceptance despite scientific evidence that the practice of smoking them is deadly. I believe that if marijuana becomes legal, it will probably be the weight of public opinion that matters again, far more than medical or scientific justifications, either way, pro or con. [This is not to say that common sense shouldn't be a factor in our thinking about public health, but the common sense as reflected in our medical prejudice about marijuana is chemically no sense.] It is interesting that society is now embracing a chemically dangerous drug and worried about a relatively safe one. I say again that it is interesting [only] to note how public opinion can change poison to water and water to poison and it really doesn't seem to make much difference what the chemical makeup is.

I do not completely believe that a government or official survey into the use of an illegal substance like marijuana could arrive at an accurate index or numerical figure indicating the extent of marijuana use in America or by Americans abroad. With all the extensive official literature on the subject, it is still almost impossible to get a vague picture of the widespread effects of the drug. This in itself demonstrates some of the haziness of most official publications concerning marijuana use. Because I represent no agency, have smoked marijuana, have been exposed to it in a variety of social climates, and because of my personal interest and investigation into the subject, I believe I have access to perhaps more realistic information about marijuana in general than any austere survey could deliver.

[It can be easily assumed that if a certain number of people are known to smoke marijuana, then a great many more smoke it that are not known about. The same assumption is naturally made in the statistics reporting the amount of drugs seized in any one year. We are certain that the actual amount that did enter the city will probably be even a hundred times the amount seized. For these reasons I think that a reasonable doubt can be mustered when confronted with any official report dealing with the extent of drug use in a specific area, such as Vietnam—just as the amount of traffic deaths that take place on an American holiday gives us no concrete information as to how many people were actually driving recklessly. Of course, this reasoning applies to whatever figures I am presenting.]

In notifying me of the scope of this testimony, the subcommittee submitted a comprehensive list of questions which address themselves to the use of marijuana by American service personnel in Vietnam. I believe that these questions cover almost all that could be of interest on the subject, so I'll confine the rest of this testimony to reading those questions and answering them as directly and completely as I can.

Included in the first question, "How extensive is the use of marijuana by U.S. servicemen in Vietnam?" was the additional question of how I arrived at the conclusions that will make up the bulk of this testimony, and how I substantiate my analysis of the situation. My year in the Republic of Vietnam was in the Army as an enlisted man with Armed Forces Radio and Television, which is an information activity of the Department of Defense. I served as a newsman and a news director for the network throughout the Republic of Vietnam. I spent six months of my year in Saigon and six months in the field. I was stationed for over two months around Pleiku in the II Corps forward area, and Qui Nhon, the large Korean concentration and logistical port on the South China Sea. I [have driven] with one other man along the breadth of Vietnam from the sea in Qui Nhon to the Cambodian border near Plei Djeraing. In my field capacity for the Armed Forces Network I visited many hospitals and waited long hours in rainy flight sheds with men from other units going in other directions. I believe that I had contact with personnel from practically every battalion-size unit in the Republic at one time or another. In working for an interservice organization my associations covered all branches of the military. I also believe that I [have seen] nearly every part of South Vietnam with the exception of some parts of the Delta. I have a great many Vietnamese friends both in the United States and Vietnam, and when I was last stationed in Saigon, I was teaching English in my off-duty time at the Vietnamese-American Association. All this is to say that I was not an average soldier in Vietnam with an average job.

The result of what I believe to be my sophistication with many aspects of Vietnam tells me that about sixty per cent of American soldiers between the ages of nineteen and twenty-seven smoke marijuana when they think it reasonable to do just that, taking into consideration their responsibilities at the moment. However, I think the figure daily approaches seventy-five per cent of the previously mentioned group as they become more sophisticated about the plant. [This may perhaps be more easily considered when it is realized that the average age and culture of the men who make up the vast majority of the combat military in Vietnam reflect exactly the same group of people in the United States who are giving marijuana the popularity that has become the reason for this hearing.] I believe for the most part that this is a relatively harmless practice, both to the military at large and to the individual soldier.

The second question refers to the obtainability of marijuana in Vietnam. Marijuana, or *Cannabis sativa,* flourishes throughout almost every portion of the world. This is true for Omaha, not to mention the jungles and plains of Southeast Asia. The easy access of marijuana to American service personnel is mostly due to the exposure of the American soldiers to the Vietnamese national at all levels of his involvement in Vietnam.

It would be best to describe the use of marijuana by service personnel in this age group as both chronic and sporadic. By this I mean that their desire or affinity to marijuana is as chronic as a Scotch liker's affinity to Scotch, but the use of marijuana may be sporadic due to the amount of time available to use it. The use of marijuana, to a user of the drug, is in amounts as normal and intelligent as the use of anything by anyone. Most intelligent people would not get stinking drunk before approaching something important. Neither would it occur to someone who smokes marijuana to get particularly high when he knows that he should not. There is no loss of judgment and the individual is left with his facility to decide for himself when to smoke and when not to.

"What is the attitude of service personnel toward the use of marijuana? Do they plan to continue its use upon their return to the United States?" The attitude of the members of the Armed Forces to marijuana is certainly a casual one. A substance that might seem momentous to a suburban family in the United States, just isn't to a sergeant first class in the Delta. The younger soldier who has friends in the States who probably smoke it is certainly as offhand about it as the rusty veteran. Soldiers who have started smoking marijuana in Vietnam may or may not continue its use when they return to the United States, although it is more likely that they will.

In answer to the question "What is the attitude of the military command with regard to the use of marijuana by service personnel?" I would say that marijuana causes an administrative problem rather than a moral dilemma or health hazard. Under the articles of the Uniform Code of Military Justice, to possess marijuana is illegal; however, this violation of the Code is noteworthy to the command as an infraction of discipline rather than through any connotation of possessing "drugs." There are too many military people for the command to deal with on a personal level, so it becomes a matter of whether control of the use of marijuana is a convenience or an inconvenience to the legal officer or company commander who has to make out the paperwork if any action is taken against members of his command. I have been among a great number of military police and legal officers who use the drug, and so another enforcement problem arises there. Also, if my figures are even nearly correct, then enforcement of the law in any total measure would mean taking legal action against tens of thousands of military personnel in a logistical area where such a thing would be impossible.

"What indications are there that the continued use of marijuana by service personnel has had deleterious effects upon the men, physically or psychologically?" I believe in many cases the use of marijuana has a psychologically beneficial effect on servicemen in a combat situation. This is not to say in combat itself, but rather in the overall mental health of a soldier thousands of miles away from home at war with strangers. It is not a depressant like alcohol, which can lead the mind into some pretty emotionally abysmal corridors; instead, marijuana is a euphoriant, which tends to lead to an attitude of serenity, a feeling of well-being and relaxation. It is certainly true that this is not the best psychological state of mind to be in when confronted with combat. Most soldiers who find themselves under the effects of marijuana in combat are either stupid and would be drunk in the same circumstances without marijuana or they are members of a resting element taken under surprise attack. It would not occur to a soldier to wear after-shave lotion on patrol in the jungle, much less to be smoking a cigarette of any kind.

"Has the use of marijuana by service personnel impaired their effective functioning as combat personnel?" I do not believe that marijuana has in any way significantly impaired the effectiveness of American combat personnel. The Viet Cong, who we know to be excellent fighters and skillful soldiers, have used marijuana almost to a man since early childhood. I've already made it clear that marijuana is used for the most part for relaxation and a soldier with any respect for his own life would never be likely to endanger that life if he thought marijuana affected his functioning. I don't think that there is anyone who is in a better position to judge whether a drug is debilitating or not than the individual himself, if, as in the soldier's case, he is asked to continue to perform a series of tasks of a highly physical nature whether he uses the drug or not. It must be added here that from all evidence at my disposal there is no indication that the effects of marijuana carry over for any great length of time after smoking. Certainly far less so than the physical effects noticeable in having too many beers the night before . . .

"Would the use of marijuana in combat units be as prevalent as in non-combat units?" It has been the military philosophy of every army since the Chinese philosopher Sung-tzu not to permit combat elements to have a great deal of spare time, either to think or worry. When American combat personnel come off patrol they generally fall asleep. When they wake up, they are generally given details or some other duty under the supervision of their superiors. For this reason support elements undoubtedly do have more spare time and thus more time to smoke the drug; however, because many support elements are in the cities and marijuana is most prevalent in Vietnam throughout the countryside, it could also be said that combat elements have more exposure to marijuana than many support groups.

"What is the attitude of the Vietnamese population and officials toward the use of marijuana? Is there extensive use of marijuana by the Vietnamese?" At present there is, as far as I know, no effective law in the Republic of Vietnam controlling the use or sale of marijuana. Though there may be some clauses in the new Vietnamese legislation involving the revenue received from marijuana, such laws are ignored to the same extent as most other civil controls in Vietnam. About one hundred per cent of the tribal people in the central-highland region of Vietnam smoke marijuana. This includes men, women, and children. Among the Vietnamese peasants throughout the countryside I believe about fifty per cent of their number use marijuana daily. These are mostly older men and women of the villages. Though marijuana may be obtained anywhere in the cities of Vietnam, its use is not as prevalent as in the field. There seems to be very much of a reverse trend in Vietnam from that seen in the United States. In revolting against their peasant background, the

young Vietnamese of the city and his intellectual counter-
part in Vietnamese government and society prefer to drink
alcohol rather than indulge in the pastimes of the common
people. Thus, as marijuana may be used in America as an
assertion of individuality, the Vietnamese youth refrain from
its use in order to establish their individuality. Geograph-
ically, more marijuana is smoked in the mountains than in
the countryside, and more in the countryside than in the
cities. However, even with this it can easily be said that marijuana is as available in Vietnam, no matter where you are, as
cigarettes are in the United States. I also believe that a great
number of officials in the Vietnamese government probably
have access to most of the proceeds from the sale of marijuana
to American personnel in the cities.

"What other drugs are available to service personnel in
Vietnam? What are their sources? Are such drugs abused? To
what extent?" Besides marijuana, opium and amphetamines
or pep pills constitute the remainder of the drugs used by
American servicemen in Vietnam. When I was serving in
Vietnam I came across absolutely no use of the stronger
hallucinogens such as LSD, peyote, or psilocybin. However,
considering the growing popularity of these drugs in America
this is no longer necessarily the case. Opium is not a favorite
of American personnel. The intelligence level of young men
in the United States military is a great deal higher than is
generally thought, and it is common knowledge to these
people that opium is a dangerous and tremendously debilitating addictive drug. Though it is readily available, opium is
used in this part of the world mostly by the Vietnamese and
Chinese equivalent of the American narcotics addict. It's
interesting to note, however, that the vast majority of Orientals who do use opium are over the age of forty. Amphetamines, however, paint quite a different picture. These pills,
related to Methedrine, are distributed by the American government to its personnel through medical officers, corpsmen,
and survival kits. The drug is very popular, especially with

the combat soldier, because it gives him a superhuman amount of energy and in this way it could be said that it is beneficial to him, but purely as a fighting machine.

"What information do you have relative to the use of marijuana in the United States? College students? Professionals? The so-called 'Hippy Subculture'?" It should be obvious to anyone who so much as reads *The New York Times* that increasing numbers of youth and adults, from every conceivable class and subculture, including police officials and narcotics agents, are beginning to experiment with the drug. To believe anything else is to display perhaps malicious ignorance of the nature of our increasingly more drug-oriented society. This society includes the sale of tranquilizers, which in America has soared to over $200,000,000 annually.

"What recommendations would you leave with the subcommittee with regard to the control of marijuana?" I concur with Dr. Goddard about penalties being far out of proportion to the nature of the crime when we sentence a user of marijuana to jail. It seems to me to be ultimately ridiculous and defeating to the philosophy behind any legal system to turn upwards of ten million or more people into criminals because of the provincial and prejudicial nature of our laws governing the use of this substance.